£1.99

A LEVEL

Questions and Answers

GERMAN

Keith Tomlins

Principal Examiner

SERIES EDITOR: BOB McDUELL

Letts

EDUCATIONAL

Contents

Introduction

HOW TO USE THIS BOOK

The aim of this book is to provide the student with the help required to reach the highest level of achievement in important examinations: A- and AS-level German or, in Scotland, Higher Grade German. The book is designed to help all students, up to and including A grade.

The *Questions and Answers* series is based on the belief that experienced examiners can provide, through examination questions, sample answers and advice, the help a student needs to secure success.

Students often find it useful to plan their revision according to some predetermined pattern, during which weaknesses can be identified and eliminated so that confidence can grow. The main purpose of many revision aids is to provide factual information which might have to be recalled in an examination. This book, while drawing attention to grammar, structures and vocabulary that need to be learnt, shows how these are put to effective use in answering examination questions. The book concentrates on the vital skill of how to **apply** your knowledge.

This *Questions and Answers* book is designed to provide:

- A unit on each of the four skills Speaking, Listening, Reading and Writing. These skills are called **Assessment Objectives** (see p.2). Each skill unit in this book includes a brief section on Assessment Objectives which outlines what exactly is being tested in the examination. Those students who will sit examination papers which combine various skills will find the individual skill sections useful by following instructions given in the Examiner's tips to various tasks. A unit entitled **Mixed Skills** brings together the skills with essay questions based upon the Listening/Reading/Speaking tasks.

- Easy-to-use **Revision Summaries** which identify important information you must understand if progress is to be made in answering examination questions. These summaries will give you vital hints on examination and revision technique. Spend some time on this introduction to each section before tackling any questions and refer back to it whenever you find it necessary.

- Many examples of **examination questions** from actual examination papers. You will be able to improve your own answers by studying the wide range of questions on different types of task together with the examiner's advice on how to approach them. In the Speaking unit there are some **Examiner's tips** to read before you carry out the tasks. In the Writing unit you will find a **sample answer** for each task type, accompanied by an examiner's commentary to highlight errors and means of improving the answer. The advice on essay-writing is also relevant to Coursework assignments.

- **Answers** to the Listening and Reading tasks with **Examiner's tips** on how to cope with the tasks.

- A **CD** which provides the stimulus material you need in order to do the Listening tasks in the book. There is also a simulated oral test on this CD. You can practise the Speaking tasks from the book before listening to German native speakers carrying out the same tasks. Hearing them will help you improve your own performance. The CD icon in the margin refers you to the relevant track numbers for the oral examination and listening tasks.

THE IMPORTANCE OF USING QUESTIONS FOR REVISION

Examination questions can help to:

- highlight gaps in knowledge: these can be revealed only when you try to apply your knowledge to a task;
- gain confidence that you can succeed: this is built up by a large amount of practice;
- get used to the various types of question used in examinations and learn how to approach these.

It can be discouraging, if you try to answer questions on your own without some help. The advantage of this book is that it provides not only plenty of actual examination questions of the different types that you are likely to encounter, but also Examiner's tips and answers to enable you to improve your performance. For details and examples of question types and how to approach them, refer to the units on the individual skills.

ASSESSMENT OBJECTIVES

Examination papers consist of Speaking, Listening, Reading, Writing and Literature/ 'Civilisation' Topics/Thematic Studies papers. The weighting of these assessment objectives or skills depends on the individual Exam Board. The nature and the amount of written Coursework also varies according to the Board.

The relevant units of this book show how to approach the various objectives, from the skill of showing comprehension of a spoken stimulus (Listening) or of written material (Reading) to the usually more demanding skill of expressing your own thoughts and feelings in speech (Speaking) or on paper (Writing). Even if you are sitting papers combining these objectives, you need to know how to do well at each individual skill. Therefore, you should read the Revision Summary at the beginning of each unit, attempt a few tasks in conjunction with the Examiner's tips, and check your answers, before following the mixed skills route through the book to do other tasks. The Writing unit also gives guidance on Literature or 'Civilisation' questions, which will also be useful for Coursework.

ASSESSMENT OBJECTIVES

The oral examination will normally take place at your school or college or a nearby Centre before the set date for the written papers. It will be conducted either by your own teacher or by a visiting examiner, depending on your own Exam Board's arrangements.

The structure and timing of the examination will depend on your syllabus, but it would usually consist of a number of the following test situations:

❶ A Reporting task.

❷ A Role Play task.

❸ An Interpreting task.

❹ Presentation of a chosen topic.

❺ Discussion of the chosen topic. The topic could be related to 'civilisation' issues (unemployment, sport, a town/village/region of Germany or German-speaking country etc.) or literary or artistic aspects (for instance books, films, paintings or musical compositions).

❻ General conversation including personal questions and discussion of current affairs.

EXAMINATION TECHNIQUE

Confidence is the key to success! This is undoubtedly the part of the A-level examination for which most candidates are very nervous, but nerves can be overcome. You should aim to go into the examination room full of confidence. To do this you need to have prepared the subject matter thoroughly and to have had a lot of practice in speaking. In addition to the practice which you have had at school, you should have spoken as much German as you can outside it, remembering that at this level you need to be able to discuss and argue, rather than just chat. Some suggestions:

- Converse in German and do role plays of the negotiation type with a friend or group of friends preparing the same examination or who have taken it in a previous year.

- Try the same with an elder brother or sister or parent who is good at German or who has sat the examination.

- Make the most of any opportunity to visit a German-speaking country to hold debates with your penfriend (if you have one) or with any other people who are prepared not only to listen to you, but to respond critically.

- Record yourself speaking on a cassette recorder and play it back to listen to yourself. Note your good points to gain confidence. Then note your bad points – hesitancy, mistakes of pronunciation or grammar, weak development of a point or confusing explanation of an idea – and try to improve on them next time. Ask somebody who knows German quite well (possibly your teacher) to listen to your recording of yourself and to give advice. You will not feel nervous in the examination room at the thought of your speaking test being recorded, as many candidates are, if you have already made recordings and listened to them.

You will be rewarded for your ability to express your opinions and feelings, to argue and defend your views, and generally to hold your own in a genuine conversation. For the top mark you would also be expected to be very accurate and to use a wide range of vocabulary, structures, and idiom (or typically German ways of saying things).

REVISION SUMMARY

WHAT TO REVISE FOR SPEAKING

As for Writing, you need to develop your **active** vocabulary and grammar. It is easier to remember the meaning of a German word when you want to show understanding of it in English for Listening and Reading. To learn how to put something into German is much harder and needs more practice, yet most students unfortunately spend less time on this active skill.

If you do not have a book in which German words suitable for Advanced Level Study are provided with their meanings, then write them down yourself, in a vocabulary book for example, ready to revise them. For Speaking and Writing cover up the German words and test yourself on translating the English into German. It is better to learn 20 a day early in your course, but if you have started your revision late, you will have to try 50 at a time. It is not helpful to do more at one go, since your brain will not take them in. Take a break, do some other work, and return to the word list later.

Individual words are of no use, unless you can form the correct language patterns with them. Many students are too obsessed with learning word-lists to the neglect of word groups and sentence patterns. For this a deeper understanding of German grammar is essential. Grammar should also be studied in small sections or topics at a time. Try for instance to tackle one by one the points in the Revision Checklist in the Writing unit of this book.

You should shut your grammar guide and see if you can jot down the main points accurately without help. Unless you can do this, you should re-read that section of grammar and test yourself again, before proceeding to the next point on the checklist.

Listen to the oral examination on the CD/cassette accompanying this book, once you have read the advice and commentary below. The tasks in this examination and those set in this book for Exam Practice include examples of the various tasks set by different Exam Boards. Check your own syllabus to see what you are required to do. Even if a task is not stipulated by your Board, it would be worth doing it to improve your oral skills. Details of how to approach the individual tasks are contained in the Examiner's commentary on the recorded tasks and in the Examiner's tips to the other practice tasks.

If you need to revise this subject more thoroughly, see the relevant topics in the *Letts* A-level German Study Guide.

ORAL EXAMINATION ON CD/CASSETTE

The examination consists of:

❶ A Reporting task.

❷ A Role Play task.

❸ Presentation of a chosen topic.

❹ Discussion of the chosen topic.

❺ General conversation including personal questions and discussion of current affairs.

The tasks for the first two sections are set out below. Read these, then study the suggested approach to them, before preparing your own answers, as if you were about to be examined.

REPORTING TASK

Sie sind seit einer Woche bei Freunden Ihrer Eltern in München. Sie haben eine englische Zeitung gekauft, und zeigen mir, der Mutter, diesen Artikel. Da ich wenig Englisch kann, bitte ich Sie, mir den Inhalt zu erklären.

UK universities prove magnet for eager European students

Donald MacLeod
Education Correspondent

BRITISH universities are proving a magnet for European students at a time when competition for places has
5　never been tougher.

Shorter degrees, better staffing and support for students. and the chance to achieve fluent English are attracting more
10　than 6,000 new students a year from the European Community — virtually double the number coming five years ago.

Ireland, Greece and Germany
15　provide the three largest groups of European students. In 1990 the Department for Education put the number of EC students here at 22,410 but em-
20　bassies believe the official statistics underestimate the influx.

There is nothing to stop British students from applying to continental universities — ex-
25　cept their lack of language skills. Enrolment is easier than in the UK, although conditions are often crowded, and they would not have to pay fees in
30　most cases.

Unlike other overseas students, those from the EC do not pay tuition fees. Universities are happy to accept good stu-
35　dents but the imbalance repre-

sents a considerable subsidy by the British taxpayer.

Britta Baron, London director of the German Academic Exchange Service, said there 　40
were at least 8 000 German students in Britain, about half of them on the Erasmus exchange programme, under which students at European universities 　45
spend part of their course abroad.

She said there was an increasing interest in studying in Britain. "They are not so hung 　50
up about where they want to study and are quite happy to go to one of the new universities."

UK universities were more attractive than those in France 　55
or Italy which had the same problems of mass higher education as in Germany. Although a three-year English degree would not be highly regarded, a 　60
master's degree gained after four years' study would be considered equivalent to a German degree taking an average of six or seven years, Ms Baron said. 　65

Oxford

ROLE PLAY TASK

■ The outline of the role-playing task is given below. During the role play you will be expected to respond to the examiner's questions as fully as possible, and to put questions of your own whenever it is appropriate. The examiner, who will play the part of the friend, may ask for any information which may be suggested by the outline.

   ■ After a working holiday in Frankfurt you are planning to return to Britain with your German friend in his/her car. He/she is keen on any novel technological achievement and wants to use the Channel Tunnel. Try and convince him/her that travelling by ferry is much more luxurious and fun: good restaurants, bars, shops, overnight cabins. You are not stuck in your car seats, can stretch your legs, it's all part of the holiday. Altogether the whole journey takes no longer, you would have a break somewhere en route anyway. It may even be cheaper. There is a wider choice of routes, you could stop and look at some places in Belgium/Holland. Besides, you might meet some interesting people. You would never use *le Shuttle*; tell your friend why.

■ Address your friend as *du*. He/she will address you as *du*.

NEAB

Preliminary advice on the Reporting task

It is not necessary to stick slavishly to the order of points set out in the English article. Instead you should try to make sense of it as a whole in order to explain it clearly to the listener. You must not translate it line for line, but give a full and clear summary. If your Board combines the Reporting and Role Play tasks into one task, where you have to make use of the German stimulus material to answer the examiner's questions or to support your views, **do not** summarise the whole of the text. Pick out and highlight the relevant areas in your preparation period and use the text selectively, knowing for what purpose you are referring to it. If you have not studied the text thoroughly, you will waste time and be unable to complete the task within the allotted number of minutes.

Preliminary advice on the Role Play task

During your period of preparation, you should first prepare your role as it is set out in this specimen task (starting with the sentence beginning: 'Try and convince ...' to the end of the printed task). You will surely find other points in favour of taking a ferry. Many candidates do this and no more. They are then tongue-tied or try to waffle when the examiner objects to their suggestions. It is obviously far better to put yourself in the shoes of the examiner and imagine what you would say to break down your own argument. Then you will probably be able to respond quickly and argue against the examiner's ideas. It is important to do this, but politely of course. It is no use just carrying on more insistently with your own views. It is a dialogue, and you must be able to listen and make comments on what is said to you, whilst still defending your own views. This is the difference between an ordinary performance (or poor performance if your argument is limited) and a really good one.

Final advice before listening

The candidate on the CD/cassette will probably have approached the tasks in a different way from the one you have prepared.

When you listen to the Reporting task, pause the CD/cassette a few times to check what paragraphs of the newspaper article the candidate is summarising and compare this to your own version.

For the Role Play task, think of the advantages of using the Shuttle, then try to find a way of rejecting these. Wait until the examiner mentions one, then pause the CD/cassette in order to put your counter-argument. Press the play button again and hear how the candidate copes.

At the end of the Reporting task, and when you listen to the Role Play, stop the CD/cassette each time the teacher intervenes with a comment or question and try to work out what you would say in reply if you were being examined. Then you can hear the response by the candidate on the CD/cassette.

Now listen to the first two sections on the CD/cassette **before** reading the commentary on them below.

Commentary on the Reporting task

Expressions used by candidate or examiner

gemäß (+ Dative)	= according to
die Erziehungsbehörde	= Department of Education
die Botschaft	= embassy
der Abschluß	= degree (in Higher Education)
die Personalausstattung	= staffing
der Zustrom	= influx/stream of people coming
entstehen (+ Dative) *durch*	= to occur (for somebody) owing to
mit Steuergeldern ausgleichen	= to pay off with tax money
die Einschreibung	= the enrolment
angeblich	= supposedly/allegedly

In the candidate's summary, notice how the first two sentences, like many others, do not start in a humdrum way with subject then verb. The candidate makes good use of a starting phrase (*Gemäß dem Zeitungsbericht* or *Nach offiziellen Statistiken …*) followed by inversion of subject and verb. He sometimes uses passive constructions: *werden … angezogen* or *müssen … ausgeglichen werden*. He employs subordinate clauses occasionally to vary the sentence pattern, including relative clauses, two with *die* and another with *von denen*, and even starts off one sentence with *Daß* to emphasise a point (that EU students pay no fees), before finishing it with the main clause.

Notice the use of the impersonal verb *mangeln* with its subject *es* (+ Dative of person, followed by *an* + Dative) in the sentence: *Außerdem mangelt es britischen Studenten oft an den nötigen Fremdsprachenkenntnissen*.

In his response to the questions, the candidate also manages to introduce a sentence with two intertwined relative clauses (relative pronouns introducing the clauses are bold): *ein akademisches Austauschprogramm innerhalb der EU,* **das** *Studenten,* **die** *daran teilnehmen, die Chance bietet …* He concludes his final answer with a subordinate clause starting with *während*.

Don't be put off by the candidate's polished performance. It is a model to aspire to, a guide to what is possible. When speaking German, English speakers have great difficulty with word order, especially in subordinate clauses where the verb has to come at the end. Without these clauses your language will be limited, so it's worth having a go at them, even if you find yourself getting tied up in knots or making mistakes at first. Keep practising!

Content of text covered by candidate

In case you got lost, the candidate has summed up the information in the following order, the numbers referring to the lines of the text:

a) 1–3 + 17–21 + 9–13 b) 6–7 + 31–37 + 8–9
c) 14–16 + 40–44 d) 50–53
e) 22–24 + 28–30 + 26–27 f) 27–28 + 24–26

You will notice that he has omitted some lines. The examiner considered that lines 4–5 were not so important, and that the point in lines 48–49 had been conveyed in other statements. However, the examiner wished to draw out the remaining information in lines 44–47 and 58–65. Since the examiner is not supposed to understand English, she has to link up with what the candidate has said and request more detail, for example about the Erasmus Programme (lines 44–47). An alternative ploy for the examiner is to pick out a name mentioned in the text and ask a question related to this. Here she spots 'Ms Baron' and wonders who she is, and what she might have had to say about the shorter period of study required in English universities (lines 58–65).

Be prepared for the examiner to ask you questions to complete any gaps in the picture or to clarify aspects of your summary. You will still score a high mark if you are able to respond quickly and fluently to queries about **minor** missing details. However, if the examiner has to draw out major points, your mark will go down.

High marks reward initiative on the part of the candidate to present the contents of the text in a concise and coherent way without translating it line by line. You may not wish to be as bold as this candidate in taking relevant pieces of information from all over the text and piecing them together. You may wish to adopt a more conservative approach, but you need to be able to group ideas in a logical arrangement. If you present a list of them in the exact order in which they appear in the stimulus text, you will find it harder to convince the examiner that you have really understood what the important points of the text are.

You will also be rewarded for fluency, both in your original summary and in responding to any of the examiner's queries, for correct German pronunciation and intonation, for grammatical accuracy and for range of vocabulary, idiom and expression.

Commentary on the Role Play task

Expressions used by candidate or examiner

der Autoreisezug	= motorail (train)
sich die Füße vertreten	= to stretch one's legs
das ist mir unheimlich	= that gives me the creeps
Unter dem Meer hätte ich große Angst	= I would be very afraid under the sea (subjunctive for 'would')
unsere Halbzeitpause	= (here) break at half-way stage
großzügig	= generous/prepared to spend a lot
auf die Strecke ... festgelegt	= limited/tied down to the ... route
eintönig	= dull/monotonous
reizvoll	= charming/delightful/attractive
riesig	= tremendously/enormously
mir zuliebe	= for my sake/just for me
überreden	= to convince

Notice the use of the conditional tense to convey a polite request and the necessary word order in the candidate's last sentence: *Ich würde mich riesig freuen, wenn du mir zuliebe auf der Hinfahrt die Fähre nehmen würdest.*

Argument presented by candidate and how he defends it

Notice the candidate gets straight to the point: he assumes that they will be taking a ferry. He knows the examiner will reply by stating a preference for the Shuttle, so he makes some prepared objections. One of these the examiner dismisses out of hand from personal experience: *Ich weiß aus Erfahrung, daß man aussteigen und sich die Füße vertreten kann.* She also mentions the 'novel technological achievement' of the Shuttle, for which the candidate is prepared from his reading of the task.

Wisely, the candidate does not dispute these two points, since he would be on a loser, but prefers instead to respond to the examiner's third comment about the thrill of being so far under the sea. His effective response: *aber das ist mir unheimlich. Unter dem Meer hätte ich bestimmt große Angst* has probably been prepared. Having countered the examiner's argument, he then boldly takes the initiative to defend his idea of taking the ferry. He uses ideas from his task sheet but also comes up with a notion of his own: a chance to practise speaking French.

The examiner claims that she has little French, so it is pointless to push this line. She then comes in with what could be a killer blow, if the candidate had not already guessed it would come fairly early in the discussion: the Shuttle saves a lot of time. The candidate's reply: *Du mußt aber Zeit für eine längere Pause einplanen* points out the need to rest in between long car journeys. The use of the words *unsere Halbzeitpause* is very apt. Having ridden out his opponent's attack, he launches forth with another prepared objection to the Shuttle: the cost.

The examiner pretends that she has money to throw around on holiday, to which the candidate appropriately quips: *Na, das höre ich gern!* You will do well to put in these spontaneous reactions. He then uses his last prepared argument: a desire to visit Holland or Belgium, which the Shuttle route would not allow. The examiner comments: *Da ist die Landschaft so flach und eintönig*, to which the candidate quickly replies: *Ich finde die Landschaft reizvoll*. You may think the examiner's description of the Dutch and Belgian landscape is apt, but you must force yourself to disagree quickly!

When the examiner turns down the chance of visiting Brussels, the candidate has exhausted all the reasonable arguments and proposes a fair compromise: they go by ferry, and the examiner can take the Shuttle on her way home when she is on her own. This meets with the examiner's approval. This will cost her more, but she has hinted earlier that cost is no obstacle.

It is important to remember that this debate is like a (friendly) contest. It is no good just sitting there riding out the blows; you have to get in some telling ones yourself. The examiner, like an amicable sparring partner, will of course allow this, wanting to make you work hard but hoping that you will win the argument in the end. However, unless you are positive and (politely) forceful, you will go down.

PRESENTATION OF A CHOSEN TOPIC

Preliminary advice

Most candidates put a lot of preparation into this. A fair number are unable, however, to make their presentation interesting, and moreover to make it **sound** interesting. A series of facts about a topic can be immensely dull. Imagine you are the poor examiner who may have to hear details of the same topic not only a few times on the same day, but also several days in a row! At the very least make sure that what you have to say is different from the material which anyone else at your school or college is going to offer. This may seem obvious, but some Centres prepare a few candidates on the same theme, and it is up to the individual to give the subject some originality.

Practise saying your presentation into a cassette recorder and listen to what you sound like. Pretend you are talking to a group of people in front of you who have come especially to listen to you. You could ask your teacher to record your teaching group with each one of you talking individually to the others during a lesson. What you must have is a sense of audience. This makes your tone of voice and your whole approach more interesting. Some pupils have had such practice but then make the mistake on the day of the examination, perhaps as a result of nerves, of treating the presentation as a set task to be carried out into a microphone, seemingly unaware of a human presence. In the examination room you must still imagine that a group of people are sitting there eager to hear what you have to say.

It helps to state in your Presentation why you chose the topic and to convey a clear interest in it. Attempt to tell the examiner why it is of interest or importance to you, if at all appropriate. You will notice that this is how the candidate starts on the CD/cassette. It does help the examiner if you cover the main points which you wish to raise later in the discussion, because s(he) will try to deal with these first before raising other issues. However, this should not degenerate into a mere list. You should try to show why you are intending to discuss them. Above all, the presentation should be coherent, lively and capable of capturing and sustaining the examiner's interest. Don't make it sound too rehearsed as if you were a well-trained parrot – a fair number of candidates sadly do this each year.

The topic chosen by the candidate on the CD/cassette relates to current affairs and problems, as will some of the topics in his general discussion. (For specific advice on topics of a literary or cultural nature, see the next section – **Discussion of the chosen topic**.)

Now listen to the third section of the oral examination on the CD/cassette **before** reading the commentary below.

Commentary

Expressions used by candidate

die Herausforderung	= challenge
die Lebensgrundlage	= the foundation of existence
die globale Erwärmung	= global warming
die Ausdehnung der Wüstengebiete	= encroachment of deserts
das Schmelzen des Polareises	= melting of the polar ice cap
der Treibhauseffekt	= greenhouse effect
die Abholzung der tropischen Regenwälder	= tropical deforestation
der Ausstoß	= discharge (of gases)
die Bedrohung	= threat
die Ozonschicht	= ozone layer
das Ozonloch (¨er)	= hole in ozone layer
die Strahlung	= radiation
eindringen	= to penetrate
das Hautkrebsrisiko	= risk of skin cancer
das Waldsterben	= death of forests
der saure Regen	= acid rain
besorgniserregend	= causing concern/alarming
hauptverantwortlich	= mainly responsible
der Sauerstofflieferant	= oxygen supplier
die atomare Verseuchung	= nuclear contamination
das Kernkraftwerk (-e)	= nuclear power station
der Landstrich (-e)	= area/stretch of land
gefährden	= to endanger
der Ölteppich (-e)	= oil slick
der Fremdenverkehr	= tourism
beseitigen	= to eliminate/get rid of
das Gipfeltreffen	= summit (meeting/conference)
erzielen	= to achieve/obtain
die Beschränkung	= limitation
die Gewässer	= inland waters (lakes/rivers)

As in the reporting task, the candidate varies his sentence structure with inversion of subject and verb, subordinate clauses, including relative clauses, and passive constructions with *werden*.
Note how, having used the verb *sein* three times in his opening remarks, he finds other verbs to avoid it: *darstellen, werden, zur Folge haben, ausgehen von*.

Ein großes Umweltproblem stellt die globale Erwärmung dar is a statement which you would probably have put the other way around: *Die globale Erwärmung ist ein großes Umweltproblem*. The candidate not only avoids using *sein* again but achieves greater emphasis. The aim is similar in his remark: *Den gleichen Effekt können giftige Chemikalien, Öl oder ähnliche Stoffe haben*. Here you would most likely have ended rather than begun with *den gleichen Effekt*.

He starts other sentences in ways which you may not have thought to adopt:

● with a verb – *Verursacht wird dieser sogenannte Treibhauseffekt*;

● with an adjectival phrase – *Hauptverantwortlich für dieses Phänomen*;

● with a comparative expression – *Anders als in Deutschland*.

Argument presented by candidate

The candidate starts by stating his chosen topic clearly – examiners can sometimes forget your topic subject or get candidates and papers muddled up. He then declares its importance not only

for him as an individual, but also for the whole of mankind: *Die Natur oder Umwelt ist die wichtigste Lebensgrundlage für die Menschheit. Wenn die Umwelt krank wird, wird auch der Mensch krank*. The examiner notes this statement and uses it as a discussion point afterwards. If some of your sentences remain fixed in the examiner's mind or stand out as ideas to follow up, it will make the ensuing conversation easier.

Specialist vocabulary related to the topic is clearly in evidence (see **Expressions used by candidate**). The most disheartening thing for an examiner (as examination reports often convey) is to discover that the candidate has not acquired this vocabulary, in which case the conversation will be limited.

The candidate introduces his major points of concern about the environment, showing the dangers of each form of pollution. He is not presenting a list of facts but stressing the threat of each form of pollution. He concludes with his opinion that politicians are not doing enough to solve the problem, and that stricter laws are needed. Your presentation makes more impact if you state your views. These should not come out of the blue but be related to, and backed up by what you have already said.

DISCUSSION OF THE CHOSEN TOPIC

Preliminary advice

NOTE: If you have chosen a work of art, music or literature, or an artist, composer or writer, the advice in the Writing section pertaining to Literature will also help you with your approach. You may wish to read the relevant part of that section now, before reading the suggestions below.

You will be expected to know the factual details thoroughly, but also to give and defend your own opinions. If other candidates at your Centre are dealing with the same work/person, they will have prepared much the same background and factual information as you. This is why it is crucial to have your own ideas and to choose your own quotations or events in the person's life to illustrate them. It is disheartening for an examiner, when the third or fourth candidate turns to the same page of a book and reads out the same lines to back up the same point. It is like playing the same cassette over and over again. However, much the examiner may admire the work/person concerned, it is **your** view (s)he is trying to discover. The examiner will be arguing against you or querying your judgements, so it is important not to assume any preconceived values in the examiner's head, but to react to what you hear the examiner say. You must listen and try to convince the examiner of the merit of the work/person. Do not be shocked if the examiner makes some provocative statements. Rather than deeming him/her to be an idiot or conveying this – there are candidates every year who are a little arrogant, or foolish – reason politely to reject the views put forward.

Check your syllabus! Some Exam Boards expect candidates in the discussion section(s) of the oral test to ask the examiner the occasional question, in order to seek his/her views. The examiner is likely to be fairly brief in reply. After all, it is the candidate's voice which should predominate on the cassette. The examiner will probably make comments which stimulate further discussion, so be sure to follow these up, rather than carrying on with what you intended to say next. It should be a proper dialogue. It would be wise to have prepared in advance some questions which you might be able to bring into the conversation. However, make sure you introduce them at the appropriate moment, and look out for opportunities to ask an impromptu question, which makes the conversation more natural.

Now listen to the fourth section of the oral examination on the CD/cassette **before** reading the commentary below.

Commentary

Expressions used by candidate or examiner

wuchern	= to grow rampant/proliferate
der Hautausschlag (∸e)	= (skin) rash
hervorrufen	= to cause/give rise to
virusbedingt	= viral/caused by a virus
auslösen	= to trigger off/produce
zustande kommen	= to come about/take place
der Überschuß (an + Dative)	= surplus (of)
betroffen	= affected
eindringen (in + Accusative)	= to penetrate
sich ausbreiten	= to spread (out)/extend
sich verbergen	= to be concealed/hidden
das Treibmittel	= propellant
verzichten (auf + Accusative)	= to give up/do without
Ersatz- (in compound nouns)	= replacement/substitute
der Laie (-n) (weak noun)	= layman i.e. non-expert
nahezu kahl (of tree)	= virtually bare/leafless
der größtanzunehmende Unfall/der GAU (for short)	= most serious accident that is likely to happen/ worst case scenario
die Kläranlage (-n)	= (here) purification plant
der Betrag (∸e)	= sum/amount of money
einzudämmen	= to contain/stem/hold back
ein Abkommen schließen	= to enter into an agreement
Verpflichtungen einhalten	= to keep commitments
mutig	= courageous
die Öffentlichkeit	= the public
der Einsatz	= intervention/action
Gesetze durchsetzen	= to carry through legislation
verweigern	= (here) to refuse to allow
die Inbetriebnahme	= the putting into operation
Sicherheitsauflagen	= safety stipulations

Again the candidate uses a number of clauses and infinitive constructions. Apart from those which you will have heard in previous sections of the oral, there are some beginning with *wo, obwohl, als ... zu, um ... zu, zu, seitdem, da, bis*.

Notice the use of the subjunctive (bold) in the expression: *soviel **müßte** uns unsere Umwelt wert sein* meaning 'our environment should be worth that much to us'. It is used later with the meaning of 'would be': *Schärfere Gesetze ... **wären** auch hilfreich*.

The adjectival phrase: *Die am stärksten betroffenen Gebiete* is quicker and avoids a relative clause with the verb *sein*, in other words: *Die Gebiete, die am stärksten betroffen sind*. Another example of this is: *Weniger stark erkrankte Bäume*.

Note the use of *es* to anticipate the subject of a sentence, instead of starting with the subject: *Es sind Kläranlagen ... nötig*. This also stresses what is needed.

In the next example *es* is omitted in order to emphasise a word (bold): ***Wichtig** ist, daß ...* (instead of *Es ist wichtig, daß ...*).

By employing a verbal noun *die Inbetriebnahme*, the candidate avoids a whole clause (which would have to include the verb *in Betrieb nehmen*).

Another stylistic touch is the use of *zwar* (here with the meaning of 'admittedly') followed by *aber*: [*Der Einsatz von Greanpeace*] *konnte die Tests **zwar** nicht verhindern, **aber** er löste weltweit eine ungeheure Protestwelle aus*.

Play the CD/cassette again and listen out for these expressions.

Argument presented by candidate and how he defends it

When asked, the candidate gives clear and relevant examples of the different types of pollution under discussion: *Wenn die Luft stark verschmutzt ist, wie zum Beispiel früher im Ruhrgebiet in Deutschland …* OR: *An der Riviera beispielsweise …*

When required to explain something, he does so promptly and directly, as with algae or the greenhouse effect. Notice that the examiner constantly returns to points in the presentation of the topic: *In der Einleitung … In Ihrem Vortrag.* This is in fairness to the candidate in order to cover all his points, but also to see whether he knew what he was talking about. This is normal procedure for the examination, for which you should be prepared.

Sometimes the examiner is deliberately provocative: *In Ihrem Vortrag sprachen Sie von Ozonlöchern. Ich habe noch keine gesehen.* OR: *Meinen Sie damit, daß ich auf meinen Kühlschrank verzichten soll?* In the first example, resist the temptation to think that the examiner is thick and explain how the hole in the ozone layer can be detected and the damage it can cause. In the second, don't become too personal but describe the alternative solution as convincingly as possible.

When twice confronted with the cost of his solutions, the candidate is ready to point out the greater cost of not adopting them! See if you can react as quickly as this, when your argument is being broken down.

You will have detected that the candidate is well aware of recent events that have a bearing on this subject, such as Chernobyl, the 'Brent Spa' and the 'Sea Empress' disasters, the French atomic tests and the Greenpeace attempts to prevent them. His relevant knowledge of the political situation in Germany is introduced to good effect at the end with his views on the Green Party. Try to keep up with current affairs, particularly in relation to your chosen topic.

The candidate is capable of putting forward his own solutions both in terms of what politicians could do and what action the individual should be prepared to take. It is no good being negative; there must be a positive side to your argument, with an indication of your own ideas. You are not supposed to be converting the examiner to your view of the world, but you are attempting to promote a lively discussion.

GENERAL CONVERSATION

Preliminary advice

The main problem for candidates is usually lack of preparation for this part of the examination. The examiner will probably expect you to explain your interest in learning a foreign language and any plans for the future, whether it be study or work. If you are merely able to give factual details on these matters, then the conversation will remain at a basic level with a correspondingly low mark. The examiner will be looking for reasons behind your decisions. Notice on the CD/cassette the questions:

Warum haben Sie gerade diese Fächer gewählt?
Wie sind Sie zu Ihrer Entscheidung über den Studienort gekommen?

It should not be too much trouble for you to think all this out in advance. Your teacher will probably have discussed these aspects in German with you in lessons. If necessary, write down your thoughts and ask your teacher, or German assistant if you have one, to listen to you talking about them, preferably with some questions to ask you.

The examiner will try to relate the discussion to Germany and may steer things this way, as in the examination on the CD/cassette, with a question about any visits you have made to a German-speaking country:

Waren Sie schon oft in Deutschland?

This will soon be followed up by a prompt of the type on the CD/cassette:

Warum fahren Sie so gerne nach Deutschland?

Your response to this will give the examiner some scope to select a general topic of conversation related to a German-speaking country.

For the candidate in our example the question that follows is about any homeless people which he may have seen on his visits to Hamburg. If the examiner chooses such a point of discussion for you, and you are unable to say much about it, make this clear straight away. It is no use floundering for a minute or two, since you do not have long to make a good impression. However, you will not score a very high mark in this section, if you have to keep turning down the topic which the examiner proposes. It would be a good idea, when declining to take up the first subject, if you pointed the conversation towards an aspect of a German-speaking country which interests you. The advice about keeping abreast of current affairs for your chosen topic applies to this section as well. It is discouraging for an examiner to find that the candidate has little or no knowledge of a German-speaking country or seems unwilling to explore it in discussion. Notice the examiner's interest in the media:

Man hört in den Medien immer wieder von vielen Obdachlosen und hoher Arbeitslosigkeit in Deutschland.

and the candidate's eagerness to show that he is up-to-date:

In den Nachrichten, wird oft über Arbeitslosigkeit berichtet. Zur Zeit soll es nach offiziellen Berichten knapp über 4 Millionen Arbeitslose geben.

AND: *Ich habe kürzlich einen Fernsehbericht gesehen, der ...*

Commentary

Expressions used by candidate or examiner

Fremdsprachen liegen mir sehr	= I have a flair for foreign languages
die Einheimischen	= the local/native people
Wirklichkeit werden	= to come true/become a reality
Spaß beiseite	= joking apart
der Studienplatz (⸚e)	= place at University
selbständig	= independent(ly)
das gesellschaftliche Leben	= social life
der Gesichtspunkt	= point of view
erholsam	= restful
der Gammler (-)	= drop-out
die Sozialhilfe	= social security payments
wegrationalisieren	= to shed (jobs) (by natural wastage)
verlegen	= to transfer
das Unternehmen	= concern/business/enterprise
Billiglohnländer	= low wage countries
kurzfristig/langfristig	= in the short term/long term
Beschäftigungsprogramme	= job creation schemes
die vorhandene Arbeit	= the jobs available
ungerecht verteilt	= unfairly allocated/distributed
Überstunden	= overtime
Personal einstellen	= to take on staff
von ... ausgehen	= to assume/be based upon
betteln	= to beg
die Altersstufe (-n)	= age-group
der Angehörige (see below)	= relative/relation
unterdrücken	= to suppress/oppress/repress
den Kontakt abreißen	= to break off contact
vertreiben	= to drive out/turn out
die Wohlfahrtsorganisation	= charity
Caritas	= (in UK) CAFOD

wohltätig	= charitable
ehrenamtlich	= voluntary/in honorary capacity
verhältnismäßig	= relatively speaking
die Kluft	= the gap
im Überfluß	= in luxury/affluence
das Existenzminimum	= subsistence level
sich (für etwas) einsetzen	= to show commitment/support (for)
die Heilsarmee	= Salvation Army
verringern	= to reduce

Note that *Obdachlose/Arbeitslose/Angehörige* are adjectival nouns. They have the same endings as an adjective would: *so der Obdachlose/ein Obdachloser/viele Obdachlose/die Obdachlosen*, with the same endings in these instances for *Arbeitslose/Angehörige*.

Argument presented by candidate and how he defends it

The candidate responds directly and promptly to the preliminary questions which were highlighted in the advice you read before you listened to this section of the recording. He always gives more than one example or reason when explaining his choice of A-levels, foreign language study, and University. His interest in Germany extends beyond the land itself and its attractions, which he is keen to point out, to the people and their qualities.

He is able to joke about the idea of making a lot of money in his future career. Try to relax! Don't become too serious or get yourself worked up. This only makes it more difficult both for you and the examiner.

We have already seen that the candidate displays an eagerness to talk about recent media coverage of the discussion topics, but he is ready to show his own first-hand experience:
Aber in Hamburg habe ich zum Beispiel viele Obdachlose gesehen, von denen manche auf den Straßen bettelten.
AND: *In Hamburg existiert beispielsweise die sogenannte 'Tafel', die Essen für Obdachlose kostenlos anbietet.*
You may have noticed that the examiner deliberately tries to play down the problem of homelessness:
Gibt es in Deutschland wirklich so viele Obdachlose, wie man immer hört?
OR: *Sind nur junge Leute von Obdachlosigkeit betroffen?*

This is merely to stimulate the candidate into a more urgent emphasis on the extent of the problem and into giving a more vivid account of what he has witnessed.

As in the topic discussion, the examiner can be provocative:
(Of the unemployed:) *Darunter sind vielleicht viele Gammler, die nicht arbeiten wollen?*
(Of the homeless:) *Die meisten sind doch bestimmt junge Leute, die von zu Hause abhauen möchten, oder?*

As in the first instance, there may be something in the examiner's tone of voice to tell you that the tongue is in the cheek. In the second remark, the *oder* is a clue that the statement can be challenged. As in the other parts of the oral, the candidate who tends to agree with the examiner on such issues, thus killing off discussion, makes life very hard!

Here, the candidate is justified in replying to the quip about young homeless people:
Nein, das ist übertrieben.

Of course, he then goes on to explain why young people – and, later, older people – become homeless, just as he reasons that the majority of unemployed people want to work.

As in the previous section of the oral, the candidate goes beyond merely saying that governments are not doing enough, in order to mention possible solutions:
Listen to the statement beginning:
Es ist sicher sehr schwer, Lösungen zu finden …
and to his later suggestion:
Ich bin wirklich der Meinung, daß die vorhandenen Beschäftigungsmöglichkeiten gerechter verteilt werden müssen.

The examiner challenges this with:
Wie stellen Sie sich das vor?
Whereupon, the candidate is ready to explain:
Überstunden sollten gesetzlich verboten werden, und mehr Teilzeitarbeitsplätze sollten geschaffen werden.

Avoid involving yourself too deeply in possible solutions, if you feel you are out of your depth. This will not count against you. However, if you have ideas, let the examiner know.

The candidate goes on to say what part he tries to play – however small – in alleviating the suffering of the victim, namely his work with the Salvation Army. It can be disappointing for the examiner to hear an account of the wonderful things that should be done in the world, only to find that the candidate has never thought about making any contribution! This does happen, so prepare to say what you do.

EXAM PRACTICE

Now that you have worked your way through the CD/cassette, you should be ready to try to perform the following tasks in conjunction with a friend or relative who speaks German. Alternatively you can work in front of a cassette recorder, taking the part of the examiner as well as that of the candidate in order to make up a proper conversation or discussion.

TASK A

Study the article below and then, **in German**, explain the main points to the examiner.

You must not translate the article but you may refer to it if you wish.

SMILE, YOU'RE ON CAMERA

By the time this magazine reaches your door, up to 250 motorists will be prosecuted each week for speeding offences using evidence from police speed cameras.

Since speed cameras were introduced in London in October 1992, there has been a 38 per cent drop in accidents overall, and more significantly, a 64 per cent drop in accidents resulting in death or serious injury.

Police are delighted by the statistics and report a 10 per cent drop in traffic speed to boot. But there is no shortage of victims for the spy cameras. One motorist was photographed speeding at 105mph in a 40mph limit. However the benefits to the majority of motorists are clear; the reduction in the volume of accidents means congestion has eased quite considerably too. Cameras were first introduced to reduce accidents at traffic-lights by photographing red light runners, such as the Granada pictured. Their success led to the introduction of the speed cameras.

NEAB

Vocabulary

strafrechtlich verfolgen (+ wegen)	= to prosecute (for)
die Geschwindigkeitsüberschreitung	= speeding
das Beweismaterial/die Beweise	= evidence
die Unfallzahl ist um 38 Prozent zurückgegangen	= there has been a 38 per cent drop in accidents
von größerer Bedeutung	= more significantly
ein tödlicher Unfall	= accident resulting in death
die Geschwindigkeit ist um 10 Prozent herabgesetzt/verlangsamt worden	= a 10 per cent drop in speed
eine Geschwindigkeitsbegränzung von 64 km/h (Kilometer pro Stunde)	= 40mph speed limit
die Straßen sind weniger verstopft/ die Verstopfung hat abgenommen	= congestion has eased
ein Fahrer, der bei Rot über die Ampel fährt	= red light runner

---

Examiner's tip Try to group points in a logical sequence as below. There is no need to translate these word for word, but you must convey the facts.

Main points to convey:

- cameras first used at traffic lights to reduce accidents; this led to speed cameras;
- 250 motorists prosecuted every week for speeding thanks to speed cameras.

Examples:

- Granada in picture; motorist doing 105mph in 40mph zone;
- speed cameras have caused 38% drop in accidents overall and 64% drop in accidents causing death or serious injury;
- speed cameras have induced a 10% drop in traffic speed;
- streets are less congested.

Study the article below and then, **in German**, explain the main points to the examiner.

You must not translate the article but you may refer to it if you wish.

TASK B

'Dirty' London sweeps critics aside as cleanest capital in Europe

The traditional national pastime of rubbishing our capital city received a jolt yesterday when London defeated Berne, Paris, Berlin and five other cities to be declared the cleanest capital in Europe.

Tidy Britain, a government-funded anti-litter campaign, sent pairs of surveyors to each of the nine capitals to measure the cleanliness of the main parliamentary, tourist and shopping and station areas.

The group's director for London, Elizabeth Allen, said the results showed the capital was cleaner than many Londoners would believe or accept.

"Our surveyors found very little litter in central London. That may sound strange, but people sometimes judge on pre-conceptions rather than the actuality," she said.

The survey covered only the centre of the capital, where Westminster council spends £15 million a year on hyper-modern cleaning techniques.

Peter Bowers, aged 59, who works as a street-cleaner for a cleaning company, is sceptical about London's litter record in the poorer outer boroughs. "I live in South London and my home area is nowhere near as nice. They keep the centre tidy for tourists."

Apart from stepping on a blob of chewing gum that stuck to my shoe, I counted 190 items of litter on Victoria Station.

The bulk of items was formed by cigarette butts – 129 of them.

George Caton, aged 19, was spotted dropping one such fag end on the floor.

"Of course I'm bothered by litter," he said, "but there's people employed for that – I'm bothered keeping them in jobs."

NEAB

Vocabulary

schlechtmachen/runtermachen	= to rubbish
eine Aktion gegen Abfälle	= anti-litter campaign
(here) *der Abfallinspektor*	= surveyor
vorgefaßte Meinung	= preconception
die Wirklichkeit/der tatsächliche Zustand	= actuality
Reinigungsmethoden	= cleaning techniques
der Straßenkehrer	= street-cleaner
(einer Sache) skeptisch gegenüberstehen	= to be sceptical (about a matter)
der Außenbezirk	= outer borough
der Großteil der Abfälle	= the bulk of items
der Zigarettenstummel (-)/die Kippe	= cigarette butt/fag end

> **Examiner's tip** Main points to convey:
>
> - surveyors sent by a litter campaign funded by British government to inspect cleanliness of nine European capitals;
> - they only surveyed main parliamentary, tourist and shopping areas;
> - survey showed London's city centre to be the cleanest despite traditional contrary preconceptions;
> - Westminster Council spends £15 million a year to clean up with ultra-modern methods;
> - street-cleaner thinks poorer outer boroughs such as his in South London are dirty;
> - reporter counted 190 items of litter including 129 fag ends on Victoria station;
> - George Caton's attitude to litter.

TASK C Sie wollen ein Jahr an der Uni in Stuttgart studieren. Sie möchten in eine Wohngemeinschaft einziehen, aber der Vater/die Mutter der deutschen Familie, bei der Sie wohnen, ist dagegen. Versuchen Sie, ihn/sie von den Vorteilen dieser Idee zu überzeugen. Als Argument könnten Sie vielleicht erwähnen:

- billig
- Selbständigkeit
- Wohnen mit Gleichaltrigen und Gleichgesinnten
- Geselligkeit

Kommen Sie zu einem Kompromiß.

Oxford

Vocabulary

eine Wohngemeinschaft	= people sharing a flat or house
gleichgesinnt	= of similar interests/outlook
die Geselligkeit	= company/companionship

> **Examiner's tip** You will, of course, prepare your defence of the views suggested above. You could expect the examiner to claim that it could be expensive, because fellow students might run up a few bills and you would be expected to share the costs. You might not get on with them, they may be lazy and exploit you, leaving you with most of the housework, shopping and cooking. Surely, a student hostel would be less risky but still provide sociability. You must effectively counter these criticisms of sharing accommodation.

■ The outline of the role-playing task is given below. During the role play you will be expected to respond to the examiner's questions as fully as possible, and to put questions of your own whenever it is appropriate. The examiner, who will play the part of the farmer, may ask for any information which may be suggested by the outline.

TASK D

■ You are on the last day of a cycling tour through the *Frankenwald*, and you are expected by your friends in Würzburg that night. Some two hours from Würzburg you hit a stone and land in the ditch. You are hardly hurt at all, but the bike is damaged. You have no tools and you cannot repair it. You go to a nearby farmhouse for help. You want to get the bike repaired. If this is not possible, find out where you could spend the night. Is there a youth hostel nearby? Could you perhaps stay at the farm? You have a tent. Where can you have a wash? You also need to contact your friends to let them know.

■ Address the farmer as *Sie*. He/she will address you as *Sie*.

NEAB

Vocabulary

an einen Stein stoßen	= to hit a stone
im Graben landen/in einen Graben fallen	= to land in a ditch
beschädigt	= damaged
das Werkzeug	= set of tools
sich verletzen	= to injure oneself
das Bauernhaus	= farmhouse
ein Zelt aufschlagen	= to put up a tent
zelten	= to camp

Examiner's tip You will be expected to explain why you are in that area of Germany, what has happened to you, and that you are not injured but can't repair your bike. Then you need to ask politely for the farmer's help. You might expect that the farmer is unable to carry out the repairs, that he has no room in the farmhouse, and that the next youth hostel is a fair distance away. You will then have to negotiate about putting up a tent in the farmer's field. Hopefully, you won't have to wash in the stream, but the farmer might be mean enough to suggest it initially. Offer to pay for the use of his facilities, especially the telephone!

TASK E Study this material on the effect of violence in films. Be prepared to discuss the material itself and any issues which may arise from it.

LÖST GEFILMTE GEWALT GEWALT AUS?

Der Nährboden für Mölln und Solingen?

Die Filme, in denen Menschen mit Kettensägen, Ninja-Sternen, Kampfpanzern und Flammenwerfern bestialisch umgebracht werden – was sonst?

from *Stern*

„... eine soziale Krankheit"

AEB

Vocabulary

die Gewalt(tätigkeit)	= violence
die Gewalttat (-en)	= act of violence
die Kettensäge (-n)	= chain saw
der Kampfpanzer (-)	= battle tank
umbringen	= to kill
der Mord (-e)	= murder
der Mörder (-)	= murderer/assassin
ermorden	= to murder/assassinate

der (Bank)Überfall (-̈e)	= bank raid
der Überfall (auf jdn)	= assault
der Überfall (auf offener Straße)	= mugging
die Notzucht/die Vergewaltigung	= rape
die Schlägerei/die Prügelei (-en)	= fight/punch-up/brawl
brandstiften/die Brandstiftung	= to commit arson/arson
seiner Phantasie freien Lauf lassen	= to let one's imagination run riot
in einer Phantasiewelt leben	= to live in (a world of) one's imagination
die Auswirkung auf die Persönlichkeit	= effect on the personality
eine Idee verwirklichen	= to put an idea into action
gefilmte Gewalt löst Gewalt aus	= violence on film triggers off violence

---

Examiner's tip The vocabulary above concentrates on the negative side, but you may wish to defend violence in films as being harmless and cathartic. If you come out against it, the examiner may pretend to feel that the amount of violence in films is exaggerated and that it is purely imaginary, so be prepared to defend whatever view you hold. You are unlikely to find the examiner agreeing with everything you say.

2 *Listening*

ASSESSMENT OBJECTIVES

The approach to Listening varies slightly from one Exam Board to another. However, the type of stimulus material will fall broadly into these headings, not all of which will necessarily be covered in your syllabus:

- short news flashes;
- advertisements;
- weather reports;
- news reports;
- other types of monologue, including telephone messages;
- discussions and interviews, sometimes quite long.

Range of tasks

A wide variety may be set on the stimulus, which may include:

- objective type tests where you are not required to produce any written German yourself but choose from German words/statements offered to you;
- sentence completion in English;
- answering questions in English, including summary;
- sentence completion in German;
- answering questions in German.

The standard of your written German

- The German you write in your answers must be recognisable without any possible confusion to a native speaker. Check that what you have written actually makes sense. It must communicate clearly.
- At least the bulk of the marks are awarded in the Listening paper for your ability to show comprehension of written German. Check your own syllabus to see which parts of the paper also carry specific 'language' marks for your ability to express yourself in German.
- In transcription tasks, your German must be perfectly accurate.

EXAMINATION TECHNIQUE

Practice makes perfect

The only solution is to have plenty of practice at each type of task and at various lengths of text. The purpose of this book is to provide the opportunity for this, as well as to help you to complete the tasks successfully.

Other possibilities are:

- cassettes available from your teacher;
- cassettes of past examinations (**but** these are expensive);
- German penfriend or friend of family;
- German-speaking radio or television via cable and satellite;
- BBC radio programmes, e.g. *Deutsch für die Oberstufe*;
- BBC/Independent Television programmes for schools, e.g. *The German Collection*.

Speed of delivery

The speed of delivery on the tape depends on your Board, but it is generally faster, if you are allowed to play the tape back yourself. Only repeated practice will enable you to get to grips with normal German speaking speed. For news reports, so often used in examinations, the speed seems paranormal. The newsreader in any language seems to be concerned with strict time limits and tends to have a very fast delivery. Don't let this faze you. Listen to German-speaking radio and television broadcasts. Recording them, if the reception is good, allows you to hear them a few times: you will need to do this to gain gradual understanding of what the German speakers are saying. This kind of listening will also help you cope with different accents: you will notice variations on the cassette accompanying this book, particularly in Listening Task S.

Dictionaries

Whether these are permitted, and what type (monolingual or bilingual), depends on your Board. Even if you are allowed a dictionary, you still have to learn the necessary vocabulary, because you will not have time to look up many words during the examination. You will need to have developed thorough and precise skills in using the dictionary, in order to be able to find the word you require in the shortest amount of time.

Playbacks

Some Exam Boards allow you to play back the tape as often as you wish, others give instructions on the paper and on the cassette about the number of playbacks you will hear.

Try tackling the tasks set out in the book according to the normal procedure for your Board's Listening test, including the number of playbacks suggested for each individual task and the use of dictionaries. If you are not able to complete a task within the number of playbacks recommended, try to listen a further time for practice rather than merely looking up the answers at the back of the book.

However, in the examination, if you have individual playback facilities, you must not dwell too long on any one extract. It is better to move on to the next and come back once you have completed the other exercises, if there is time. If you have a revolution counter on your cassette recorder, it helps to note down the number for the start of each extract for later reference.

Similarly, if you are limited to the number of playbacks stipulated by the Board, don't panic if you miss or fail to understand a word or phrase. You may catch it on the next playback. If you do have to leave a question blank or unsatisfactorily answered, because the tape is moving relentlessly on, just concentrate on the next question each time. Imagine you are a golfer attempting to win the Open: it's the next shot which counts, so forget the dreadful errors!

No transcript for the Listening recordings has been included in this book. This is to prevent you in desperation from turning the tasks into Reading exercises. If you are really stuck, follow the Examiner's tips which appear with the answers, or work back from the answer and (even if you have to use a dictionary) try to pick out the corresponding words in German which you ought to have heard. It is vital that you are able to distinguish their sounds.

To obtain a copy of the transcript for these Listening exercises, please send a stamped, self-addressed envelope (A4) to Letts (address on inside front cover).

The references in brackets [ ] in the advice which follows are to examples in the tasks, e.g. [Task B2/3] means Task B questions 2 and 3. There are sometimes several examples, but one or two are given, so that you can understand the nature of the advice given.

Length of extracts

● You will be expected to cope with a variety of different extracts, some so short that they seem to be over before you have really tuned in [Task C], some dauntingly long [Task R and Task T].

REVISION SUMMARY

- Because an item is short, it is not necessarily easy, since a lot of information can be condensed into few words [Task C]. Even in a short extract there can be redundant material, so that the material needed for your answers has to come from very little text [Task A].

- In longer texts there may be some sentences which you can safely ignore between questions [Task K]. For longer texts [Task N onwards] you will have to retain quite an amount of material in your head (unless you wish to keep stopping the tape, assuming your Board allows this), so it is vital to train yourself in making mental notes as you listen.

- Summary questions [Tasks J/K/N4/S] can prove difficult, because you have to note down a continuous succession of points, without individual questions which could be used as markers to understand the development of the text [Contrast Task O Section A with Section C].

The topic being discussed

Extracts will usually deal with syllabus topics which you will have covered in class. Perhaps you will be extremely familiar with some of these areas. However, avoid guessing what is said from your previous work on a topic. This is a common pitfall. The facts or opinions stated might be the opposite of what you expect [B2/3].

The question wording

- Pay close attention to this. It should be obvious at this level that there is a distinction between 'When?' and 'Where?', but such words are often confused in the heat of the examination [D1].

- Beware of answering two-part questions too hastily, thus missing the second part [D5 Who … **and why?**].

- Greater subtlety is required at A-level and this can cause problems with questions in German. If you are asked to complete a sentence, pay attention to the word which starts the continuation clause: *weil* calls for a reason, *wenn* for a conditional response [E2/E3].

- In open-ended questions, if you read *Was hält er von?*, you are requested to state a person's opinions and not the facts behind them. The same applies when you are completing sentences such as *Hilde ist der Meinung, daß …* [R8].

The number of marks available

The number of points you give must match the mark indication in the margin. If only two details are required, don't waste time writing a list in the expectation that the Examiner will sift through it to find the right response [O1]. Some Boards will not allow this and only the first two answers offered are marked. On the other hand, if a high mark is to be awarded, make sure you provide enough detail. [Summary questions J/K/S, but note also N4].

Transposing the German sentence

When answering in German you often face the problem of transposing the sentence you hear to the format required for the answer [A4; E2/3]. It is essential to learn how to paraphrase in German (see the Reading unit for help). If you are unable to do this fairly quickly when dealing with a written text, you have little hope of achieving it while you are listening.

Appropriateness of your answer

- If you have to complete a grid, only a minimal answer, as short as possible to be relevant and convey the meaning, will be needed. A sentence is unnecessary [A1–A5/I2].

- Where you have to fill in a gap, ensure not only that the sentence made up in this way has the correct meaning, but that the right part of speech is used [G1/2 – verbs; G3 – nouns; L Section A first gap – preposition + noun]. Copying down phonetically what you hear without understanding it will make nonsense of the answer [A2].

- In open-ended questions where the whole answer has to be made up, you would be surprised how many candidates jot down a jumble of odd words which they have picked up and hope the examiner will construe them. Rather than trying to translate English notes back into German, which is a well-tried recipe for disaster, it does help if you take notes in German, but they must be made coherent.

WHAT TO REVISE FOR LISTENING

Vocabulary

For Speaking you learnt your active vocabulary, working from English into German. Now you need to work the other way around. Your passive vocabulary should be larger than your active one, since this is how the mind works. When revising German words, remember synonyms for them as well, so that you are also working from German back into German. Use a monolingual dictionary for this purpose. This will help you with your answers in German as shown in the paragraph above entitled: **Transposing the German sentence**.

Here are some further revision hints, based on the problems candidates have in performing examination tasks.

Problems caused by faulty understanding of German

Numbers: on the whole A-level candidates know individual numbers, but they often fail to hear them in sequence, as in dates or statistics. Hearing *neunzehnhundertneunundsiebzig* candidates can give such diverse answers as: 1997/1990/1970/1917 none of which is correct. The common error (as in 1997) is to get the right numbers individually but not in the right order [J last point]. Statistics are also tricky [F/Q4], particularly where you have to select the correct one from a few mentioned [H]. The German use of the comma as a decimal point must also be remembered [D6].

Beware of false friends

- Some words deceive us by seeming to be close to English words by sound: in weather forecasts *heiter* may seem to mean 'hotter', whereas it means 'bright'. *Schwindel,* as well as being what it sounds like (a 'swindle'), is also 'dizziness'. You can draw up your own list of these, which may prevent you from falling into a trap in the exam.

- Other words appear to mean what we want them to mean, but have a different sense in German: *ausschlafen* can in today's context of the homeless be misunderstood as 'to sleep out', but it is used for having a long sleep (*draußen schlafen* = to sleep out).

Words with slightly similar sounds but different meaning

ehrlich	= honest(ly)	*ehelich*	= relating to marriage/marital
Unsinn	= nonsense	*umsein*	= to be up	*umsehen* = to look around
Vorname	= first name	*vornehm*	= distinguished
Bürgerkrieg	= civil war (heard as *Bergkrieg*, a non-existent word, = war in mountains)		

These are words which have actually been confused in examinations, as are the following examples which you can work out for yourself:

Paralyse/Parallele	*Berge/Burgen*	*ein Schweizer/ein Weißer*
Fahrrad/Radfahren	*Formen/Reformen/Formeln* [G4]	*kommunale/Kriminale* [K4]
Lehre/Lehrer [R4]		

REVISION SUMMARY

Use of prefix to change meaning

As in the example of *aus* (see **Beware of false friends**) which can mean 'out' as in *ausgehen*, the prefix can cause havoc. Note how the inseparable prefixes *ent-/ver-/miß-* radically alter the meaning of a verb:

In these examples *miß-* has the value of 'mis-' in English:

trauen – mißtrauen   verstehen – mißverstehen.

Note also: *gelingen* = to succeed   *mißlingen* = to fail

kennen	= to know		
erkennen	= to recognise	*verkennen*	= fail to recognise
lernen	= to learn	*verlernen*	= to unlearn/forget
achten	= to pay heed to	*verachten*	= to despise
fahren	= to travel	*sich verfahren*	= to lose one's way
erben	= to inherit	*enterben*	= to disinherit
sprechen	= to speak	*entsprechen*	= to correspond to [P1]

Separable prefixes also need care:

schließen	= to lock	*aufschließen*	= to unlock [see also B1/3]

Sometimes the same prefix and verb combination can have different meanings:

auskommen: Sie kommt gut mit ihren Brüdern aus   = she gets on well with her brothers
auskommen: ich kann mit hundert Mark nicht auskommen = I can't manage on DM 100.

umziehen   = to move house   *ein Kind umziehen* = to change a child's clothes
*sich **um**ziehen*   = to change (one's clothes)
*sich um**ziehen***   = to become overcast (of sky) [Task C].

Note the different stress in these words, shown in bold, as this, together with the other words in the context, will help you work out the meaning. When the stress is on the prefix it is separable, so the word order or past participle formation is also a clue to the meaning:

*Ich ziehe mich **um**/habe mich **umge**zogen*   = idea of changing clothes
Der Himmel umzieht sich/hat sich umzogen   = idea of overcast

Use of tenses

This is harder to detect in Listening than in Reading comprehension, but can be crucial to the answer. [B1 – even if you understand the words, the wrong tense will cost you the mark]. When you have to formulate the answer in German, the tense must be clear. If you write: *genimmt*, the examiner will not be sure whether you mean present *nimmt* or past *genommen*.

Singular or plural

German plurals can be tricky and need to be learnt thoroughly. Sometimes the singular and plural forms of a noun are identical, in which case there are other grammatical pointers:

*mit **einem** Ausländer*   = with a foreigner (Note the article)
*mit Ausländer**n***   = with foreigners (Note dative plural ending)

Use of negatives

These are often overlooked – some examples from the tasks:
nicht [B2/I2/P1/R2]
noch nicht [F3]
nicht unbedingt (= not necessarily) [K5]
niemand [O1]
kein [R8/T9]
the prefix *un-* [I4/Q9/Q10]
the negative value of *erst* (= not until)
Other examples: *nie, nichts, weder … noch, nicht nur … sondern auch.*

Qualifiers and quantifiers

These are often ignored or mistranslated. Make sure you listen out for and understand the following:

ein bißchen, (ein) wenig, ein paar, einige, mehrere, viel(e), ganz, sehr, so, ziemlich, zu, etwa, ungefähr, außerordentlich, äußerst, echt, recht, richtig, wirklich.

Comparatives

mehr, weniger, eher, lieber … (als) – missing these can be fatal.

● *Er ist mehr/eher faul als dumm* = He is more lazy than stupid/He is lazy rather than stupid. Don't confuse this construction with *sowohl … als/wie auch …* = both … and …

● *Eher/lieber will ich sterben, als ihn heiraten* – the speaker is determined **not** to marry the person in question.

REVISION SUMMARY

If you need to revise this subject more thoroughly, see the relevant topics in the *Letts* A-level *German Study Guide*.

LISTENING TASKS

- Each item is recorded only once on the CD/cassette. You will hear a double tone at the end of each item and a single tone between any sections of an item.
- Unless otherwise advised by the instructions at the beginning of each task in the book, play the whole item through twice, ignoring section breaks.
- Before listening to the recording, make sure you read the rubric and the questions carefully and know what is expected of you. This is what you must do in the examination room.

TASK A

In the first item you will hear what happened when Kathy Watts, an Olympic gold and silver medallist in Barcelona, paid a return visit to Spain.

Ergänzen Sie auf **deutsch** folgende Notizen über den Fall Kathy Watts.

Lesen Sie jetzt die Notizen.

Und jetzt folgt der Bericht.

1 Nationalität		(1)
2 Sportart		(1)
3 Grund ihrer Verhaftung		(1)
4 Verkehrsmittel nach Madrid		(1)
5 Inhalt ihres Koffers		(2)
6 Grund ihrer Freilassung		(1)

Cambridge

TASK B

In this item you will hear the main points of the evening's news. State in **English** what you are told about the following.

Look at Questions 1–4.

Und jetzt folgen die Nachrichten.

1 The Central Bank

.... (2)

2 The atomic power station at Chernobyl

.... (1)

3 The German Minister of Health, Horst Seehofen

.... (2)

4 The explosion at an office block in Hamburg-Lokstedt

.... (1)

Cambridge

You will find this task easier if you pause the recording to think and to write down your answer. You may have to listen more than twice.

Das Wetter. Wo sind die folgenden Wetterverhältnisse zu finden? Ordnen Sie die Buchstaben der richtigen Region zu.

TASK C

TRACK 8

A bedeckt und regnerisch

B Wolken mit Regenschauern

C vereinzelt Regen

D Wolken

Region	Buchstabe	
1 Nordwesten	....	(1)
2 Schleswig-Holstein	....	(1)
3 Westen	....	(1)
4 Alpen	....	(1)

Oxford

You will hear some weather details and then some news flashes.

Answer the following questions in English.

TASK D

TRACK 9

1 Where will the fog patches be persistent?

.... (2)

2 What temperatures are forecast?

.... (1)

3 Who is paying a visit to Germany?

.... (2)

4 Where will they be visiting after flying to Berlin?

.... (1)

5 Who has been protesting and why?

.... (2)

6 How many crimes were recorded in Germany last year and how many of these were solved?

.... (2)

7 What types of crime increased in Germany last year?

.... (2)

ULEAC

TASK E

Sie hören jetzt einen Ausschnitt aus einem Interview mit einem Blutspender.

Ergänzen Sie die Sätze.

Lesen Sie jetzt die Sätze 1–4.

1 Ich verbringe viel Zeit

.... (1)

2 Ich fühle mich verpflichtet, Blut zu spenden, weil

.... (1)

3 Ich brauche Blut, wenn

.... (1)

4 Heutzutage ist das Rote Kreuz so nett, daß es

.... (1)

Cambridge

You hear the following items of statistical interest on a news magazine programme.

True or False?	TRUE	FALSE
1 $2\frac{1}{2}$ million Germans are in need of treatment for drug addiction.	☐	☐
2 6 million Germans are in need of treatment as a result of their smoking habit.	☐	☐
3 There are no precise figures for gambling and eating disorders.	☐	☐
4 Alcoholism is not primarily a male disorder.	☐	☐

Oxford and Cambridge

In the following item you will hear a report about the Chinese government's intention to open Tibet to the outside world.

Füllen Sie die Lücken in den folgenden Sätzen auf **deutsch** aus.

Lesen Sie jetzt die Sätze 1–5.

Und jetzt folgt der Bericht.

1 In Zukunft wird Tibet mit anderen Ländern .... können. (1)

2 Man wird auch von Tibet direkt nach Peking, Kathmandu und Hongkong

.... können. (1)

3 Die chinesische Regierung hofft, es werden viele ....

und... nach Tibet reisen. (2)

4 Deng Xiao-Ping hat versucht, ...

.... einzuführen. (2)

5 Anfang des Jahres hat er .... besucht. (2)

Cambridge

TASK H

You hear a short report about the police and crime in Germany.
Fill in the missing information.

According to the figures released by the Interior Ministry in Schwerin the police in Mecklenburg-Vorpommern are no worse than in any other Federal state. In a force of some .... at present only two are under investigation because of .... According to a spokesman, in 1993 only .... officers were subject to investigation or disciplinary measures. There were a mere eight cases of .... About .... bicycles are stolen a year in the Federal Republic. The German Association of .... reckons this is costing their members some 160 million DM a year, the result of which is increased .... Bicycles stolen outside the house, say on the street, are not covered unless .... (8)

Oxford and Cambridge

TASK I

Suzanne spricht über ihre Erfahrungen in Schulen in Deutschland und in Schottland. Mache Notizen über das, was sie sagt!

Du sollst erwähnen:

1   was sie gemacht hat, das ein bißchen außergewöhnlich war

    .... (1)

2   wie die Lehrer in Klassen 5 und 6 waren

    .... (2)

3   warum die Realschule ihr gefallen hat

    .... (2)

4   welche Probleme sie am Anfang auf dem Gymnasium hatte

    ....

    ....

    .... (3)

SEB

You should listen to this three times, if necessary.

In dem folgenden Ausschnitt aus einer Rundfunksendung geht es um die berühmte historische Glocke in Bad Hersfeld.

Summarise what we are told about the Lulus bell, giving as much detail as possible about its peculiar shape, its age and its history.

....

....

....

....

....

....

.... (7)

NEAB

In this item you will hear a German sixth former explaining why he enjoys working on the school newspaper and talking about the **kinds** of article it carries.

Make a list in **German** of five of these.

1 .... (1)

2 .... (1)

3 .... (1)

4 .... (1)

5 .... (1)

Cambridge

TASK L

Listen to the whole item once, ignoring the single tone between the Sections, then hear each Section separately twice.

Der folgende kurze Radiobericht handelt von einem Unfall in einem chemischen Werk in Frankfurt.

Ergänzen Sie die Textlücken mit den fehlenden Wörtern.

Section A

Frankfurt am Main: Der Chemieunfall am Montag beim Hoechst-Konzern hat Folgen.

Nach Angaben der Feuerwehr meldeten sich bisher über dreißig Menschen

.... , die über Augenreizungen, Kopf- und   (1)

Atembeschwerden klagen. Allerdings mußte keiner von ihnen stationär

....   (2)

Section B

Die Staatsanwaltschaft Frankfurt ermittelt derzeit gegen die Firma Hoechst wegen des

.... (2)

Bei dem Unfall waren rund 2,5 Tonnen der giftigen Chemikalie O-Nitroanisol ins Freie gelangt.

NEAB

TASK M

Follow the same listening procedure as for the previous task (Task L).

Der folgende kurze Radiobericht handelt von einer Firma, die HIV-infizierte Blutprodukte verkauft hat.

Ergänzen Sie die Textlücken.

Section A

Der jüngste Aids-Skandal zieht ....   (2)

Insgesamt sollen in Deutschland mehr als 1 000 Krankenhauspatienten Blutprodukte der

wegen illegaler HIV-Tests geschlossenen Firma UB-Plasma in Koblenz erhalten haben.

Section B

Das .... will jetzt den Ländern   (1)

konkrete Unterlagen .... ,   (2)

um die Rückverfolgung von eventuell HIV-infizierten Präparaten zu ermöglichen.

NEAB

Listen now to an interview with Dilara, a Turkish girl who has lived all her life in Germany. Here she discusses her experiences at school at the local *Gymnasium* in Germany.

Und jetzt hören Sie ein Interview mit Dilara, einer Türkin, die ihr ganzes Leben in Deutschland verbracht hat.

Answer the questions in **English**.

TASK N

1   Explain how Dilara feels about her own position culturally as a member of a Turkish family having lived all her life in Germany.

.... (2)

2   What particular problem is there for Turks living in Germany when they leave school?

....

.... (2)

3   When the topic of racial hatred was raised, what annoyed Dilara about her friends' attitude to her at school?

....

.... (2)

4   Relate the incident which so shocked Dilara when she was researching her school project on racial hatred.

....

....

....

....

.... (6)

Cambridge

TASK 0

Listen to the whole item once, ignoring the single tone between the Sections, then hear each Section separately twice.

Answer the questions in **English**.

Es folgt nun ein Ausschnitt aus einem Bericht über 'Singles', d.h. Menschen, die allein leben.

Section A

1 Name two advantages of living alone, according to the speaker.

....

.... (2)

2 What question does the speaker ask about the reason why people live alone?

....

.... (2)

Section B

3 What example of the freedom enjoyed by a 'single' is given by the speaker?

....

.... (2)

Section C

4 Summarise what is said in this section about the change in public attitudes over the past fifteen years.

....

....

....

.... (4)

NEAB

Jetzt hören Sie ein Interview mit einem jungen deutschen Studenten, der Zivildienst statt Kriegsdienst leistet.

Beantworten Sie die folgenden Fragen auf **deutsch**.

1 Nennen Sie die Gründe, warum Achim den Kriegsdienst nicht leisten wollte.

....

....

.... (3)

2 Was sagte der Herr aus Köln zu Achim?

.... (1)

3 Warum wollte Achim im Krankenhaus arbeiten?

....

.... (2)

4 Seit wann arbeitet er schon da?

.... (1)

5 Was kann Achim nicht machen?

....

.... (2)

6 Was für einen Tag mag er nicht?

.... (2)

7 Warum hat Achim „keine leichte Zeit"?

....

.... (2)

Cambridge

TASK Q

You will find this task easier if you pause the recording to think and to write down your answer. You may have to listen more than twice.

Geiseldrama in Celle.
Sind die folgenden Aussagen richtig (R) oder falsch (F) laut dem Hörtext?

		R	F
1	Das Fluchtauto der Geiselnehmer wurde in der Nähe von Celle gefunden.	☐	☐
2	Bevor sie geflüchtet sind, haben die Kidnapper eine Geisel auf freien Fuß gesetzt.	☐	☐
3	Man fühlt sich in der Polizeieinsatzzentrale in Celle etwas entspannter als beim Beginn des Geiseldramas.	☐	☐
4	Das Geiseldrama hat schon 92 Stunden gedauert.	☐	☐
5	Es ist im Moment verboten, genaue Einzelheiten über den Fall bekanntzugeben.	☐	☐
6	Die Kidnapper halten wahrscheinlich eine Geisel noch gefangen.	☐	☐
7	Die Gangster sind mit den drei Geiseln aus dem Celler Gefängnis geflüchtet.	☐	☐
8	Der Mann im Fluchtwagen bei Großburgwedel war angeblich gebunden.	☐	☐
9	Das hat der Pressesprecher der Celler Kriminalpolizei inzwischen bestätigt.	☐	☐
10	Man weiß, wohin die Gangster geflüchtet sind.	☐	☐
11	Was die Gangster verlangten, wurde ihnen gegeben.	☐	☐
12	Unter anderem verlangten sie einen Fernseher.	☐	☐

Oxford

You will hear an interview with a female apprentice car mechanic.

Sie hören jetzt ein Interview mit einem weiblichen Kraftzeugmechanikerlehrling.

Beantworten Sie die Fragen 1–6 auf **deutsch** und vervollständigen Sie die Sätze 7–12 auf **deutsch**.

Lesen Sie jetzt die Fragen und die Sätze 1–12.

Sie hören jetzt das Interview.

Section A

1 Was sagt Hilde zu Kunden, die glauben, daß Kfz-Mechaniker ein Männerberuf sei?

....

.... (2)

2 Warum staunen so viele Kunden über weibliche Mechaniker wie Hilde?

.... (1)

3 Wofür hat sie sich als Kind interessiert?

.... (1)

4 Bei wem hat sie nach der Schule gearbeitet?

.... (1)

5 Wie lange dauerte ihr Praktikum bei Hansen?

.... (1)

6 Warum konnte sie zwei Wochen lang nicht zur Arbeit kommen?

.... (2)

Section B

Vervollständigen Sie die folgenden Sätze auf **deutsch**.

7 Der Interviewer meint, daß es unweiblich sei,

.... (2)

8 Hilde ist aber der Meinung, daß es nicht unweiblich sei, und daß

....

.... (2)

9 Hilde wird .... behandelt. (1)

10 Nur wenige Mädchen wählen gewerblich-technische Berufe, weil

....

.... (2)

11 Eine Freundin von Hilde wollte ....

.... , aber ihr Vater

.... (2)

12 Hildes Freunde sagten, daß ....

.... (1)

Cambridge

TASK S

You will find this task easier if you pause the recording to think and write. You may have to listen more than twice. Your answers can be in note-form. Give 14 details.

Listen Sie die Hauptcharakteristika der Rhätischen Bahn auf Englisch auf.
Beispiel: It is a railway with a one-metre gauge.

1	**2** ....
3	**4** ....
5	**6** ....
7	**8** ....
9	**10** ....
11	**12** ....
13	**14** .... (14)

Oxford

Listen to the whole item once, ignoring the single tone between the Sections, then hear each Section once separately.

You hear an interview with two members of a team who specialise in giving advice over the phone to the unemployed. Answer the questions in **English**.

Section A

1 What prompted the founding of the service in 1983?

....

....

.... (3)

2 What became necessary after a certain time?

.... (1)

3 What sort of psychological problems are associated with unemployment?

.... (3)

Section B

4 In what way do men behave differently from women when they come for advice?

.... (1)

5 How do men view unemployment?

.... (1)

Section C

6 What great advantage does the telephone service offer to the unemployed?

.... (1)

7 How has the service become known all over Germany?

.... (1)

8 What is the usual difference between the service they offer over the phone and the face-to-face advice they give in the office?

.... (1)

9 Give an example which illustrates the way in which their service is completely confidential.

.... (1)

Oxford and Cambridge

3 *Reading*

ASSESSMENT OBJECTIVES

Some A-level papers are by nature, and sometimes also by title, 'Reading and Writing' papers. Only the Reading exercises are given in this unit. Exercises set for Writing have been included in the next unit.

A variety of tasks are set in Reading papers. Some are 'objective' tests, such as, for example, multiple choice, finding a word in the set passage which has the same meaning as one given in the question, matching sentences, putting captions to pictures, grid or sentence completion using a given list of words. Here you are not required to produce any words of your own in either English or German, but to select and/or match given material in relation to what you have read.

There will also be some answers to be written in English or a translation or summary to be done in English.

Answers in German may involve merely finding your own word to insert in a blank space. Others will involve using complete German sentences of your own, in which you will not be rewarded for simply lifting material from the targeted area of the stimulus on the paper. You will have to paraphrase what you have read. Some questions expect you to give a German definition of a German word or phrase.

As you will have noted in the Listening unit, if you are required to answer in German, your German has to be accurate enough to convey the correct information. All, or at least the bulk of the marks are awarded in the 'Reading' questions of the paper for your ability to show comprehension of written German. Check your own syllabus to see which parts of the paper carry specific 'language' marks for your ability to express yourself in German.

This unit gives you practice in the various types of exercise that A-level candidates are expected to be able to carry out. Check your own syllabus to see which types are usually set by your own Exam Board, but by all means have a go at all those given here. They will extend your vocabulary and help develop your manipulation of German. More elaborate use of language exercises will be dealt with in the Writing unit.

EXAMINATION TECHNIQUE

Some preliminary advice is given in this introduction about the more difficult tasks: Paraphrasing, Translation, Summary. Refer to the Examiner's tips on the individual tasks for more detail and for advice on other types of task. (The comments made in the **Examination Technique** section of the **Listening** unit in the paragraphs '**The question wording**' and '**The number of marks available**' also apply to Reading.)

Paraphrasing

You need to build up your knowledge of German synonyms. Look for books such as the Duden *Sinn- und Sachverwandte Wörter* in a library. A German–German dictionary is also an essential tool.

Practise rewording passages you are reading into your own German. You will notice that German writers, like those of any other language, avoid using the same words more than they absolutely have to. They employ synonyms instead of repeating themselves. This means that you can save a lot of sweat by doing some detective work on the text you are reading.

List the different ways in which the writer has said the same thing, then you can juggle these around when you are trying to paraphrase individual sentences. Reading Tasks H/I/J show how you can do this with examination texts. Merely by using words given to you in the text (and in other questions!) you can answer a question with as many of your own words as possible. It is perfectly legitimate for you to do this. What you must not do is to lift words from the area of text targeted by the question. So, if the question is clearly on lines 1 to 3, you are allowed to convey the meaning of those lines by borrowing synonyms used in any of the other lines of the text. (See Examiner's tips to Task I Part (i) Questions 2/5/6 and Task J Part (i) Question 2).

Alternatively, you can alter the parts of speech used in the original German. You can, for example, change nouns to verbs (See Examiner's tips to Tasks H Part (ii) Questions 1/4, I Part (i) Questions 1/9, J Part (i) Questions 1/4/7) or verbs to adjectives (See Examiner's tips to Task I Part (i) Questions 7/9). You can break up compound words into their constituent parts and use these in your answer (See Examiner's tips to Tasks I Part (i) Question 10, and J Part (i) Question 1. Sometimes, you will be forced to draw on your own bank of synonyms (see Examiner's tips to Tasks I Part (i) Questions 4/9/10/11 and J Part (i) Question 7).

Sentences can be turned around. You can change a passive construction with *werden* into an active one with a subject borrowed from the text or the question (See Examiner's tip to Task I Part (i) Question 11) or with the subject *man* (See Examiner's tip to Task I Part (i) Question 5). If you are confident about your German try doing the opposite, which is harder, switch an active sentence into the passive form (see Examiner's tips to Tasks I Part (i) Question 2 and J Part (i) Question 1).

See also: **Transposing the German sentence** in the **Examination Technique** section of the Listening unit.

Translation into English (Tasks K/L/M/N)

This can cause difficulty for various reasons. It is easier to hide lack of vocabulary in comprehension exercises, because you are not tested on every word in a stimulus text. When translating, you must know every word thoroughly, at least in the section of the text you are required to render in English.

There are a few key principles to remember:

● Read all the lines you have to translate, before starting the translation. If it is a section of a text upon which you have been working for other Reading exercises, you still need to reconsider these lines. You may well have skipped over them, for it is unlikely that any previous question would have been set specifically on them. If it is an entire text which you have to translate 'unseen', there is all the more need to ensure that you really understand what the German passage is saying. Sadly, a number of candidates show that they have not really grasped the overall meaning.

● You must be faithful to the passage you are translating. Each word or phrase is there for a purpose and must be rendered. This is not a gist comprehension exercise or summary where you can just pick out the main points. It is a faithful replica in English, like a kind of mirror image of the original. Some candidates find it useful to write each bit of a sentence down in English as they read through the German, so as not to miss out a word. What they have written at the end adheres to the German text, but, of course, does not sound very natural in English. This is a good way to start with the tasks provided in this book. If you are really adept at translating you will be able to jump around in the German sentence picking out the words in the order in which you need to put them to make a proper English sentence. But that only comes with practice.

● If you have made a rough word for word version, you must then make sense of this and polish it into good English style. Your final text must flow like a normal piece of English and not sound like a translation. Most candidates are found wanting to a greater or lesser degree here. They write things which, if they read them in a calmer moment, they would laugh at.

● Re-read your final version in order to tidy up any errors of English and to check for any possible omissions from the original German text.

The Examiner's tips to Reading Tasks K/L/M/N give practical examples of the methods of translation suggested here.

Summary on English (Tasks O/P)

This is a quite different skill from that of translation. Some candidates make the mistake of giving every word of the original German, as if they were translating. This never works because of the word limit stipulated on the paper.

A few key principles:

- Check the maximum number of words permitted in your summary. Then do a rough calculation of the number of words in the passage set. Do this by counting the number of words in the first three lines and dividing by three to find an average number per line, then multiplying by the number of lines in the passage. This shows you how many words you need to cut out. Some tasks require more pruning than others.

- As for translation, make sure you read the passage thoroughly and understand what it is conveying, above all its key points.

- Jot down in note-form each important point as it occurs to you as you go through the passage again. Check quickly through once more, in case you have left something vital out. Now count how many words you have used. You should have some spare at this stage.

You should then be able to write your notes out in continuous prose conveying precise and clear information. The use of continuous prose rather than a series of random notes will take up the words you left spare. Your answer should contain the required points without exceeding the word limit.

**If you need to
revise this
subject more
thoroughly,
see the relevant
topics in the
Letts A-level
German
Study Guide.**

WHAT TO REVISE FOR READING

Essentially this is the same as for Listening. Refer to the following paragraphs in **What to revise for Listening**: **Vocabulary, Use of prefix to change meaning, Use of tenses, Singular or plural, Use of negatives, Qualifiers and quantifiers**. Remember also the points made in the **Paraphrasing** advice earlier in this unit.

READING TASKS

Once you have read the stimulus text, you may find it helpful to read the Examiner's tip before answering the questions. The tips help, where necessary, with vocabulary and guide you towards the correct answers. If you are feeling more confident, you can have a go on your own and then check the answers and tips to see where and why you may have the wrong answer.

Baby kam im Taxi zur Welt

TASK A

Lesen Sie den Artikel.

Wer hat was in dem Text gemacht? Kreuzen Sie die richtige Person oder Personen an. Nummer 1 ist als Beispiel schon gemacht worden.

WER ...	Barbara Zimmerer	Wolfgang Zimmerer	Jennifer Zimmerer	Paul Paschke	Die Taxifirma
1 ... rief die Taxifirma an?	X				
2 ... schickte Paul Paschke?					
3 ... war von zu Hause weg?					
4 ... versuchte den Arzt zu alarmieren?					
5 ... wußte, was zu tun war?					
6 ... hatte die Geburt seines Kindes miterlebt?					
7 ... lieferte Mutter und Kind ab?					
8 ... freute sich enorm über das Baby?					

[7 Punke]

45

Köln: Baby kam im Taxi zur Welt

Fahrer als Geburtshelfer Mädchen kam viel zu früh

Von DETLEV SCHMIDT

exp Köln – **Ausgerechnet war der Geburtstag für den 5. November, doch daran hielt sich das Mädchen nicht. Gestern morgen setzten bei Mutter Barbara Zimmerer plötzlich die Wehen ein. Sofort alarmierte sie das Taxi- und Mietwagenunternehmen Joisten. Die schickten Fahrer Paul Paschke, selbst Familienvater. Und der wurde wenig später zum Geburtshelfer. Denn 500 Meter vor der Klinik wurde das Mädchen im Mietwagen geboren.**

Vater Wolfgang Zimmerer war gar nicht zu Hause gewesen, als die Wehen einsetzten. Deshalb fuhr Barbara alleine in die Klinik. Unterwegs versuchte der Fahrer über Funk einen Arzt zu alarmieren.

Doch das klappte wegen der Katastrophenschutz-Übung der Stadt nicht mehr rechtzeitig. „Alles nicht weiter schlimm. Gottseidank war ich bei der Geburt meines Kindes dabei und wußte damit, was zu tun war."

Wenige Minuten nach der Geburt lieferte der Fahrer Mutter und Tochter wohlbehalten in der Klinik ab. Und am Nachmittag holte Vater Wolfgang die beiden schon wieder nach Hause. In Begleitung von Töchterchen Jennifer (3), die sich riesig über ihr kleines Schwesterchen freute. Einen Namen für das kleine Mädchen haben die überraschten Eltern noch nicht: „Darüber wollten wir uns erst in den nächsten Tagen Gedanken machen."

Erschöpft aber glücklich: Barbara Zimmerer freute sich mit der kleinen Jennifer über das Schwesterchen, das im Taxi zur Welt kam.

Geburtshelfer: Taxifahrer Paul Paschke   Fotos: Pio

Read this passage and answer in English the questions which follow it.

ANALPHABETEN
Drei bis vier Millionen Deutsche können weder lesen noch schreiben.
Viele schämen sich, ihre „Behinderung" zu offenbaren.

Die Frau im Supermarkt hat Schweißtropfen auf der Stirn. Sie sucht verzweifelt im Regal nach weißen Zuckertüten mit blauer Schrift und
5 rotem Löffel. Als ein anderer Kunde vorbeikommt, nimmt Simone Soth wahllos eine Schachtel und legt sie in den Einkaufswagen. „Bevor die Leute es merken, kaufe ich lieber etwas
10 Falsches", sagt sie.

Was die Leute nicht merken sollen: Simone Soth, 34, kann weder lesen noch schreiben. Sie kennt zwar die einzelnen Buchstaben, ist aber nicht
15 fähig, sie zu einem Wort zusammenzusetzen.

Wie Simone geht es ungefähr drei bis vier Millionen Deutschen über 15 Jahren. Man kann genauere Zahlen
20 nicht nennen, denn die meisten Analphabeten versuchen mit allen Mitteln, ihre „Behinderung" zu verbergen.

Die meist genützten Methoden:
25 Mal haben sie angeblich ihre Brille vergessen, mal gehen sie mit verbundener Hand zum Amt. So füllen in der Behörde, der Bank, dem Postamt meist andere die Formulare
30 für sie aus. „Man hilft eher einem behinderten Menschen als einem Dummen", sagt Simone Soth.

Simone arbeitet seit fünf Jahren als Köchin in einem Altenheim. Nur der
35 Chef weiß von ihrer „Behinderung", wie sie es nennt. Jeden Tag geht sie voller Angst zur Arbeit—„Angst davor, doch einmal etwas aufschreiben zu müssen". Denn dann müßte sie eine
40 Kollegin um Hilfe bitten, „und das wäre so, als müßte ich mich vor anderen Leuten nackt ausziehen".

Fast jeder, der in Deutschland heute als Analphabet gilt, hat die Schule
45 besucht und das Abc gelernt. „Daß es trotzdem so viele nicht können, liegt oft an zu großen Klassen", sagt eine Expertin. „Woher sollen Kinder, die Probleme haben, dann noch Hilfe
50 bekommen, wenn die Eltern zu Hause keine Zeit haben—oder vielleicht selbst weder lesen noch schreiben können?"

Simone Soth ist nur selten zur Schule gegangen. Als zweites von
55 zwölf Kindern mußte sie sich um ihre Geschwister kümmern. Mit 14 zog sie von zu Hause aus, fand eine Stelle als Putzfrau und lernte schließlich ihren Mann kennen. Lange Zeit ahnte er
60 nichts. In Restaurants bestellte Simone stets Mineralwasser und Schnitzel, „denn das gibt es überall". Erst nach zwei Jahren fiel ihm auf, daß sie auch nie in die Fernsehzeitschrift schaute,
65 und hielt ihr auffordernd ein Buch vor die Nase: „Lies!" Da mußte sie ihre Behinderung zugeben.

Heute bedauert Simone Soth, daß sie ihren drei Kindern nie etwas
70 vorlesen konnte. „Ich habe mir Geschichten ausgedacht und im Buch ab und zu die Seite umgeblättert. Die Kleinen haben es nie gemerkt." Und die Hausaufgaben später wurden erst
75 überprüft, wenn abends der Papa kam.

Analphabeten fühlen sich sehr oft von einer Person abhängig und haben wenig Selbstvertrauen. Wenn sie jedoch Kurse besuchen, um ein
80 bißchen Lesen und Schreiben zu lernen, wächst dieses Selbstvertrauen und auch der Wunsch, mal etwas alleine zu machen, nicht immer kontrolliert zu werden.

85 Die meisten Analphabeten besuchen Kurse aus Angst, keinen Arbeitsplatz zu finden, oder den Kindern bei den Hausaufgaben nicht helfen zu können.

Seit ein paar Monaten geht auch
90 Simone Soth zweimal pro Woche abends zur Volkshochschule. Inzwischen kann sie ihre Adresse schreiben und einfache Texte lesen.

Nun möchte sie ihrer ältesten
95 Tochter in *Koblenz* eine Postkarte schreiben. „,Herzlichen Glückwunsch, meine liebe Claudia—Deine Mutti' soll draufstehen", sagt sie. „Und keiner schreibt mir die vor. Das mache ich
100 ganz allein. Damit meine Tochter auch mal auf mich stolz sein kann."

1 How do people like Simone cope in everyday situations such as shopping and dealing with the authorities?

....

....

....

.... (4)

2 (a) Why are so many people in Germany illiterate?

....

....

.... (3)

(b) What are the reasons for Simone's illiteracy?

....

.... (2)

3 What did she do to hide her 'handicap' from her husband and children?

....

....

.... (3)

4 (a) Why do some illiterate people decide to learn to read and write?

.... (1)

(b) What additional, less obvious benefits do they find?

....

.... (2)

(c) What is motivating Simone to learn to read and write?

....

.... (2)

SEB

Read this text and answer in English the questions which follow it.

> **Auf abenteuerliche Weise reisten Hunderttausende von deutschen Jugendlichen diesen Sommer durch Europa, häufig ohne Ziel, manchmal ohne Geld. Schattenseite des Rucksack-Tourismus: Schwierigkeiten und Kriminalität in den fremden Ländern.**
>
> "Irre, einfach irre", fand eine Fünfundzwanzigjährige aus Frankfurt ihre Reise nach Spanien, und verrückt genug war es schon.
>
> Sie hatte sich mit mehreren Freunden zur Fiesta in Pamplona verabredet, Treffpunkt Café Tropicana. Vom Autobahn-Kreuz, der bevorzugten Tramperstation im Rhein-Main-Gebiet, ging es dann los. 36 Stunden später, nach einem Dutzend Etappen in schaukelnden Citroën-Enten und klapprigen Lieferwagen, stand sie dann tatsächlich vor dem Tropicana, übermüdet und hungrig, aber pünktlich. Doch das blieb dann auch ziemlich das einzige, was klappte.
>
> Ein Dach überm Kopf war nicht mehr zu bezahlen, nachdem ihr im Festgewühl Bargeld und Papiere gestohlen worden waren. Und die spanische Sonne, die doch bei Tag und Nacht scheinen soll, machte sich selten. In Kälte und Regen kampierte sie mit ihren Freunden zumeist im Freien.
>
> Ganz schön chaotisch verlief schließlich auch die Rückreise. Nichts war mehr zu essen, die letzte Cola wurde geteilt, und beim Handgemenge mit einem Lastwagenfahrer, der aufdringlich wurde, zertrümmerte sie ihre Armbanduhr. Trotz allem fand sie die Reise wunderschön.
>
> Hunderttausende junger Bundesbürger, oft minderjährig, haben sich diesen Sommer auf den Trip durch Europa gemacht und überschwemmen mit Schlafsack und Rucksack die Strände und Metropolen. Sie sind meist knapp bei Kasse und leben von Weißbrot und Dosenbier, fallen gelegentlich unter die Räuber, und die meisten haben auch noch ihren Spaß daran. Das Kennenlernen und gemeinsame Erlebnis macht diese Art des Reisens für sie so attraktiv, wie natürlich auch der Preis!

1 How did the 25-year-old from Frankfurt make her way to Pamplona?

....

....

.... (3)

2 In what state was she on her arrival?

.... (2)

3 What difficulties did she encounter while on holiday in Spain?

....

....

.... (3)

4 What happened to her on her way back?

....

.... (2)

5 Give details about the type of young person embarking on a holiday of this nature.

....

.... (3)

6 Why do young people find this type of holiday so attractive?

....

.... (2)

NICCEA

Read this passage and answer in English the questions which follow it.

Im Westen auf der Arbeitssuche

Stefan hat wieder einmal schlecht geschlafen. Zweimal haben ihn in der Nacht Polizisten geweckt. Aufwachen. Aufstehen. Papiere zeigen. Der 23jährige kennt die Fragen, und die Beamten kennen seine Antwort. Er ist Tourist, und es sei nicht verboten, in Hamburg ein polnisches Auto zu parken. Die Polizisten wissen, daß er lügt. Doch sie haben andere Sorgen auf St. Pauli, als ihn um das bißchen Schwarzarbeit zu bringen.

Stefan quält sich vom Fahrersitz und beginnt zu frühstücken. Ein Milky Way, das er sich aus dem Kofferraum geholt hat, ein Schluck Aldi-Limo aus der Dose. Das Gas für den Kocher ist ausgegangen. Die Konserven aus Polen sind verzehrt, ein paar andere Lebensmittel noch zwischen Reservereifen und Klopapier deponiert. Er kriecht mit Kopfschmerzen aus dem Blech. Er muß ständig daran denken, die Polizisten könnten ihn wieder nach Hause schicken. Wo er zwar ein Bett hat, aber keine Arbeit als Mechaniker findet. In Hamburg gibt es wenigstens Drecksarbeit.

Morgens um fünf läuft Stefan zum Baumwall am Hafen, einem der Plätze in der Stadt, wo sich ein Arbeitsstrich etabliert hat. 30 Polen lauern dort stundenlang am Straßenrand. Handwerker in Pritschenwagen rollen langsam an ihnen vorbei, um das Angebot des Tages in Augenschein zu nehmen. Ein Wink, die Männer beugen sich durch heruntergedrehte Fenster. Für zwei, fünf, acht, zehn Mark die Stunde steigen sie ein. Wer Pech hat, gerät an einen Betrüger. Stefan kennt Kollegen, die monatelang umsonst geschuftet haben. Auch ihm wäre das fast einmal passiert. Aber da ihm die Adresse seines Auftraggebers bekannt war, konnte er ihn aufsuchen und mit Prügeln bedrohen. Anders geht es nicht, sagt Stefan. Wo sollten sich Illegale beschweren? Bernhard Fasz vom Arbeitsamt entdeckte eine Baustelle in Uetersen bei Hamburg, wo Polen Dachgeschosse ausbauten. Der Vorarbeiter schraubte jeden Abend die Griffe der Türen ab, hinter denen die Illegalen über Nacht eingesperrt wurden. Geschlafen wurde auf Matratzen zwischen Bauschutt. Tagsüber durfte nur einer die Baustelle zum Einkaufen verlassen.

Vor vier Jahren war Stefan zum ersten Mal in Hamburg. Mit dem Motorrad, 24 Stunden ohne Pause, von der polnisch-russischen Grenze bis an die Elbe. 1300 lange Kilometer. Dreimal ist er diese Strecke mit dem Motorrad gefahren, siebenmal mit dem Auto. Bezahlt vom ersten Schwarzgeld. Bei Schwerin haben ihn voriges Jahr Jugendliche auf einem Rastplatz genötigt, etwas zu Adolf Hitler zu sagen. Hitler gut, hat Stefan gestottert. Seitdem hält er nicht mehr in Ostdeutschland.

1   What has happened to Stefan during the night?

....

....

.... (4)

2 Why is he forced to have a cold breakfast?

.... (1)

3 What is his greatest fear?

.... (1)

4 Explain the process by which young men like Stefan get jobs.

....

....

....

.... (4)

5 (a) What example of bad luck is given?

.... (1)

(b) How did Stefan avoid this happening to himself?

.... (1)

6 Describe fully the conditions under which the Polish workers in Uetersen were living.

....

....

....

.... (5)

7 Why does Stefan no longer break his journey in eastern Germany?

....

....

.... (3)

AEB

Read this passage and match up the parts of the German sentences which are given after it.

Die Arbeit einer Schwester der Sozialstation

Human alt werden - in den eigenen vier Wänden

Selbständig sein Bett verlassen, sich waschen oder anziehen kann der 97jährige nicht mehr. Seine Frau kann ihn nicht mehr heben und stützen. Mit 86 Jahren gehört sie schließlich nicht mehr zu den Jüngsten und steht selbst etwas wackelig auf den Beinen. Es gibt keine Tochter oder Schwiegertochter, die sich um die beiden Alten kümmert. Dennoch: Sie leben in ihren eigenen vier Wänden, einem Bauernhaus aus dem 17.Jahrhundert.

Täglich kommt eine Pflegerin oder ein Pfleger der Sozialstation Grenzach-Wyhlen ins Haus. Heute ist es Schwester Marlis. Als erstes legt sie Holz im Ofen nach. So etwas wie eine Zentralheizung gibt es in dem alten Bauernhaus nicht. Dann wechselt sie bei der alten Frau einen Verband. „Wenn es doch nur mit dem Laufen besser ginge", klagt sie leise. Anschließend hievt Schwester Marlis den alten Mann aus dem Bett und wäscht ihn. Das Wasser hat die alte Frau schon vorher auf dem Ofen heiß gemacht. Während sie das Frühstück fertig macht, versorgt die Mitarbeiterin der Sozialstation den Mann. Sie wäscht ihn, verarztet wunde Stellen, zieht ihn an, kämmt und rasiert ihn. Heute stutzt sie ihm den Bart.

Der Platz in einem Pflegeheim würde hier in der Gegend zwischen 4800 und 6300 Mark kosten. Nur 750 Mark im Monat kosten dagegen die 25 Hausbesuche der Plegerinnen oder Pfleger von der Sozialstation. Mehr Einsätze zahlen die Krankenkassen derzeit nicht.

Die alte Frau ist froh, daß sie noch in ihrem Haus leben kann. Glücklicherweise hat sie zwei unverheiratete Söhne, die im Haus wohnen. „Die legen den Vater am Abend wieder ins Bett und kümmern sich am Wochenende um ihn. Ich pack' ihn halt nimmer." Ihre Jungs sind es auch, die Holz hacken und den Garten in Schuß halten. „Bis vor zwei Jahren haben wir die Sachen noch selbst gemacht", erzählt die Frau.

Wenn Schwester Marlis da ist, dann hat sie für eine halbe Stunde jemanden zum Reden. Sie spricht von ihrem Leben, von der Zeit, als es auf dem Hof noch Kühe und Schweine gab, als Acker und Weinberg bewirtschaftet werden mußten. Gerne spricht sie von ihren Kindern, der einzigen Tochter, die ausgewandert

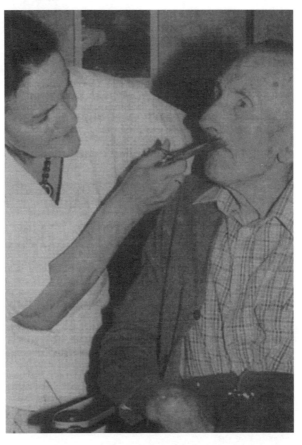

Die Schwestern und Pfleger der Sozialstation tun mehr für „ihre" alten Menschen, als sie zu verbinden und anzuziehen
Bild: kb

ist, und dem verheirateten Sohn, der in Bayern lebt, und natürlich den beiden Söhnen im Haus. Vertrautheit herrscht zwischen dem Ehepaar und der Schwester, die „irgendwie fast zur Familie gehört".

Mittlerweile hat sie den Alten zum Frühstücken an den Küchentisch gesetzt. Es drängt die Zeit. Immerhin wollen 15 bis 20 alte Herrschaften zwischen 7 und 13 Uhr versorgt werdcn. Bei den einen muß die examinierte Krankenschwester Katheter ziehen oder Spritzen verabreichen, andere muß sie baden oder neu betten und lagern.

NB Druckfehler im 3. Absatz: Plegerinnen = Pflegerinnen

Human alt werden

Welche Satzteile gehören zusammen? Vorsicht! Es gibt mehr Endungen als Sie brauchen. Nummer 1 ist als Beispiel schon gemacht worden.

[12 Punkte]

1	2	3	4	5	6	7	8	9	10	11	12	13
B												

Anfänge

1 Dieser alte Mann kann nicht mehr von seiner Frau versorgt werden, …

2 Die beiden alten Menschen halten sich gewissermaßen für selbständig, …

3 Wasser muß auf dem Ofen geheizt werden, …

4 Die alte Frau beschwert sich, …

5 Die alte Frau kann das Frühstück machen, …

6 Diese Pflege ist für die Krankenkasse viel besser, …

7 Das alte Ehepaar kann sich jetzt ausruhen, …

8 Bis vor 2 Jahren haben die beiden alles für sich selbst machen können, …

9 Schwester Marlis muß nicht am Wochenende und am Abend kommen, …

10 Die alte Frau freut sich, wenn die Schwester Marlis kommt, …

11 Nur 2 Söhne sind noch zu Hause, …

12 Für Schwester Marlis ist die Zeit knapp, …

13 Schwester Marlis' Arbeit ist vielseitig, …

Endungen

A … weil sie zwischen 7 und 13 Uhr fünfzehn bis zwanzig alte Menschen versorgen muß.

B … weil sie jetzt dazu zu alt ist.

C … weil Schwester Marlis eine Verwandte der Familie ist.

D … weil sie noch die Kraft dazu hatten.

E … weil eine Tocher ausgewandert ist und ein dritter verheirateter Sohn in Bayern lebt.

F … weil sie in ihrem eigenen Haus leben können.

G … weil sie sowohl medizinische als auch Haushaltsarbeit tun muß.

H … weil Schwester Marlis für den alten Ehemann sorgt.

I … weil das Haus keine Zentralheizung hat.

J … weil sich dann die zwei Söhne um ihren Vater kümmern.

K … weil sie billiger als ein Platz im Pflegeheim ist.

L … weil sie dann eine Gesprächspartnerin hat.

M … weil ihre zwei Söhne die schwere Arbeit tun können.

N … weil sie Probleme mit dem Gehen hat.

Oxford

Read this passage and fill in the blanks in the German sentences which follow it.

Marketing-Tage der Uni Passau – Annette Peltzer erfolgreich

Kind, Küche und Karriere müssen nicht kollidieren

Von C. Haug

Passau.
Kind, Küche und Karriere? Ist das für eine Frau in einer Führungsposition vereinbar?
Für Annette Peltzer, Marketing-Managerin eines mittelständischen Unternehmens in Köln und Absolventin der Universität Passau, schon.

Die dynamische Frau bekleidet weiterhin ihre Position als Managerin und zieht gleichzeitig ihre beiden ein- und zweijährigen Kinder auf. Möglich wurde das durch eine besondere Vereinbarung mit ihrem Arbeitgeber während der Zeit ihres Mutterschutzes. „Ausgerüstet mit Computer, Telefax und Telefon führe ich den Großteil der Bürotätigkeit von zu Hause aus", erklärte Frau Peltzer bei der 3. Neuburger Marketing-Tagung auf Schloß Neuburg, für die sie dieses Thema als Vortrag vorbereitet hatte. „Ich empfange sogar meine Geschäftspartner zu Hause - da wird dann halt im Wohnzimmer mit dem Kundenberater der Werbeagentur über die Prospektgestaltung diskutiert", ergänzte Frau Peltzer.

Diese besondere Vereinbarung mit dem Unternehmen beruht auf großem Vertrauen, das sich Frau Peltzer innerhalb ihrer vierjährigen Tätigkeit als Marketing-Leiterin bei dem Hersteller von Basismaterial für elektronische Geräte erarbeitet hat. Außerdem ist für sie ihre Karriere lange nicht zu Ende: „Meine Karriere fährt vorübergehend nur im kleinen Gang." Sobald die Kinder im Kindergarten sind, möchte Frau Peltzer noch einmal voll durchstarten:
„Wahrscheinlich werde ich mich dann als Messeorganisatorin selbständig machen."

Auf jeden Fall riet sie den Zuhörerinnen, sich zuerst ein Standbein im Beruf zu schaffen, bevor sie an Nachwuchs denken.

Die über 100 Teilnehmer bei den 3. Neuburger Markteting-Tagen waren Diplomanten der Betriebswirtschaftslehre mit Schwerpunkt Absatzwirtschaft und Handel und Absolventen der UniPassau. „Wir wollen mit dieser Veranstaltung den Erfahrungsaustausch zwischen Theorie und Praxis, die Begegnung zwischen Studenten und Absolventen fördern", erklärte Professor Dr. Helmut Schmalen, Passau.

Kind, Küche und Karriere müssen nicht kollidieren

Ergänzen Sie die Lücken in dieser Zusammenfassung des Textes, um zu zeigen, daß Sie den Zeitungsartikel richtig verstanden haben. Manchmal paßt ein Wort aus dem Zeitungsartikel.

[15 Punkte]

Es ist durchaus möglich für eine Frau in einer leitenden Position, Kind, Küche und Karriere

zu [1]... . Annette Peltzer, die [2].. Marketing-

Managerin eines Betriebes in Köln, hat ihr [3].. zu Hause, wo sie

auch gleichzeitig ihre zwei jungen Kinder [4].. .

Durch moderne [5]..................................... hat sie sowohl zu ihren Kunden als auch zu ihren

Geschäftspartnern schnell Kontakt. Diskussionen mit Kollegen finden im [6].......................... statt.

Nach einer [7]... Tätigkeit bei ihrer jetzigen Firma traut man ihr zu, ihre

[8]... zu Hause gut zu verrichten.

Bei der Marketing-Tagung hat sie einen [9]... über ihre Tätigkeit

gehalten. Im Moment kommt ihre Karriere nur im [10]................................... Tempo voran.

Später möchte sie [11]... weiter arbeiten, indem sie Messen organisiert.

Sie ist davon überzeugt, daß eine Frau erst an Kinder [12]... sollte,

wenn sie sich in ihrer Karriere [13]................................... fühlt. Die Marketing-Tage hatten den

Zweck, Studenten mit [14]................................... Leuten in Kontakt zu bringen, damit sie

Theorie und Praxis miteinander [15]... können.

Oxford

TASK G

Read this text and answer the questions which follow it.

Von Fax-Geräten, Faxen und eiligen Liebesschwüren

Die meisten großen und wichtigen Erfindungen des Fortschritts haben auch viel Elend über die Menschheit gebracht. Das gilt für das Feuer und das Rad in grauer Vorzeit ebenso wie für den Reißverschluß und die Kassen in Supermärkten, wenn die Bon-Rolle gerade gewechselt werden muß. Von der Erfindung, Einführung und epidemieartigen Verbreitung des Fax-Gerätes ist ähnlich Widersprüchliches zu vermelden.

Ich gehöre wirklich nicht zu denjenigen, die das Kind mit dem Bade ausschütten und lauthals stöhnen, nun hätten sie das Faxen aber dicke. Doch was da täglich auf den Redaktionsschreibtisch quillt, das hat schon so beträchtliches Volumen angenommen, daß man nur mühsam die Spreu vom Weizen trennen kann.

Denn natürlich hat jeder, der in eine solche Apparatur investierte, nun auch beträchtliches Interesse, sie zu nutzen. Einmal, um die Anschaffungskosten abzuarbeiten, ferner ein bißchen anzugeben und schließlich wohl auch, um Porto und Verpackung des Briefversandes zu sparen.

Also mischen sich munter wirklich wichtige, brandeilige, blitzartige Mitteilungen, Einladungen oder Manuskripte mit schlichtem Unfug, mit ochsenfroschartig aufgeblasenen Meinungsbekundungen, Weltverbesserungsvorschlägen und weiteren fixen Faxen direkt für den Papierkorb. Gibt es eigentlich keine freiwillige Selbstkontrolle für Faxgerätebetreiber? Ich will mal so sagen: Das schnelle Fax ist wie so manches in unserer Zeit eine Bereicherung, die zugleich auch eine zeitliche Verknappung mit sich brachte (– dem Computer, unserem Sklaven und Chef, darin nicht unähnlich).

Nur für zwei Arten der bisher per Brief betriebenen Kommunikation eignet sich die Faxerei nicht. Das sind Liebesbriefe und anonyme Schreiben. Letztere, schandbare Exemplare der feigen Meinungsblubberei würden sich durch die Kennung des Absenders jederzeit entlarven. Gut so! Und auch der Austausch von faxpostalischen Zärtlichkeiten verbietet sich aus mancherlei Gründen.

Dieter Strunz

Berliner Morgenpost, 24.10.93

(i) Explain **in German** what the author means in paragraph 2 (lines 13–21) by:

1   das Kind mit dem Bade ausschütten

.... (3)

2   lauthals

.... (2)

3   sie [haben] das Faxen aber dicke

.... (3)

4   die Spreu vom Weizen trennen

.... (2)

(ii) Which words or phrases in the text most nearly correspond to the following:

1   Misere .... (1)

2   konträr .... (1)

3   Umfang .... (1)

4   Briefmarken .... (1)

5   dringend .... (1)

6   Beispiele .... (1)

Oxford and Cambridge

TASK H Read this text and answer the questions which follow it.

KARIN L.

Nach der Trennung mußten mein Sohn und ich uns ein ganz neues Leben aufbauen – ohne jegliche Hilfe des
5 Vaters. Inzwischen können Julius und ich ein fröhliches und liebevolles Leben führen. Mehr Rechte würden dem Vater meines Sohnes noch mehr Möglichkeiten geben, unsere Harmonie
10 immer wieder empfindlich zu stören. Auch meine ohnehin schon eingeschränkte persönliche Freiheit würde dadurch noch vermindert. Die Verantwortung für Kinder liegt immer
15 noch bei uns Müttern. Deshalb brauchen wir nach der Trennung Unterstützung.

UWE J.

Die Szenerie im deutschen
20 Nichtehelichenrecht halte ich für pervers und menschenverachtend. Aus der Sicht des Kindes ist die Familie eine Lebensgemeinschaft aus Kind, Mutter und Vater. Ich kann nicht
25 begreifen, woher wir im Trennungsfall das Recht nehmen, den Vater ohne Not zu entfernen. Wenn man davon überzeugt ist, daß dieser psychosoziale Kosmos zu einer gesunden
30 Entwicklung der Liebes– und Beziehungsfähigkeit eines Kindes gehört, dann kann es nur einen Gedanken geben: Wie sichere ich dem Kind diese Kontakte?

35 ### CHERYL B.

Ein Kind ist kein Objekt, an dem man Anteile kauft und Nutzungsrechte erwirbt. Ledige Mütter erziehen unter extremen sozialen, finanziellen und
40 emotionalen Belastungen. Ein Mann, dem auch nur halbwegs am Wohl seines Kindes liegt, wird bemüht sein, die Mutter des Kindes mit Anstand zu behandeln. Er wird versuchen, ihren
45 Beitrag zu würdigen und ihre Situation nicht noch weiter zu erschweren – schon allein deshalb, weil er dem Kind nicht nützt, wenn er dessen Mutter nervlich fertigmacht, sie finanziell nicht unterstützt und mit ihr im Kriegszustand 50 lebt. Die Gentechnik muß noch Fortschritte machen, ehe die Mutter sich gänzlich ausradieren läßt – bis dahin müssen Männer den lästigen Umweg über eine Frau ertragen, wenn sie 55 Kinder haben wollen.

BRITTA G.

Als meine Eltern sich getrennt haben, war ich sieben Jahre alt. Damals ist der Kontakt zu meinem Vater fast gänzlich 60 abgebrochen. Dabei hatte ich nie das Gefühl, daß er austauschbar ist. Heute arbeite ich mühevoll verschüttete Erfahrungen aus den Jahren auf, in denen ich mit meinem Vater 65 zusammengelebt habe. Ich hatte Erlebnisse mit ihm, die prägend waren. Ein Vater ist nicht einfach 'wegzuschneiden'. Rechte für nicht verheiratete Väter mögen ein kleiner 70 Schritt sein, Beziehungen zwischen Kindern und Vätern ernstzunehmen. Komplizierter und wichtiger ist es, daß die Männer ihr Selbstverständnis verändern, damit aus Zeugern und 75 materiellen Versorgern Väter werden, die Lust auf Kontakt zu ihren Kindern haben.

KARL F.

Väter sollten bei der Reform des 80 Gesetzes mehr Rechte bekommen, wenn sie dauerhaft in häuslicher Gemeinschaft mit ihrem Kind und der Mutter leben. Dann dient dies auch den Interessen des Kindes; darauf kommt 85 es an! Wer fernab von Mutter und Kind lebt, braucht nicht mehr Rechte. Er würde nur die Entwicklung des Kindes stören. Der einfachste Weg ist immer noch, die Mutter des Kindes zu 90 heiraten. Dann haben die Kinder auch Väter, die nicht nur egoistische Besitzrechte geltend machen, sondern ihre Verantwortung übernehmen.

DIE WOCHE 21/10/93 (adapted)

(i) Explain the following sentences in **English**.

1 Auch meine ohnehin schon eingeschränkte persönliche Freiheit würde dadurch noch vermindert. (KARIN L.) (Zeilen 11–13).

....

.... (3)

2 Ich kann nicht begreifen, woher wir im Trennungsfall das Recht nehmen, den Vater ohne Not zu entfernen. (UWE J.) (Zeilen 24–27)

....

.... (3)

3 Ein Mann, dem auch nur halbwegs am Wohl seines Kindes liegt, wird bemüht sein, die Mutter des Kindes mit Anstand zu behandeln. (CHERYL B.) (Zeilen 40–44).

....

.... (3)

4 Die Gentechnik muß noch Fortschritte machen, ehe die Mutter sich gänzlich ausradieren läßt – bis dahin müssen Männer den lästigen Umweg über eine Frau ertragen, wenn sie Kinder haben wollen. (CHERYL B.) (Zeilen 51–56).

....

.... (3)

(ii) Beantworten Sie bitte die folgenden Fragen in ihren eigenen Worten auf deutsch.

1 Warum könnte Karin L. meinen, daß ihr Mann das Recht auf Kontakt zu ihrem Sohn nicht verdient hätte?

....

.... (3)

2 Warum findet Uwe J. die jetzige Situation pervers?

....

.... (3)

3 Warum versucht Britta G. Erinnerungen an ihren Vater wachzurufen?

....

.... (3)

4 Welchen komplizierten Schritt will Britta G., daß Männer machen sollen?

....

.... (3)

5 Warum will Karl F. nicht gleiche Rechte für alle Väter befürworten?

....

.... (3)

Cambridge

TASK I   Read this passage and answer in German the questions which follow it.

Wie grün ist Ihr Einkaufskorb?

Hand aufs Herz: Wenn Sie am Freitag nach Ihrem Einkauf den Supermarkt verlassen, denken Sie dann jemals daran, was mit der Verpackung Ihrer Lebensmittel geschieht? Die meisten von uns werfen unseren Müll gedankenlos in den Mistkübel. Dann wird er abgeholt und verschwindet aus unserem Blickfeld. Aber er bleibt uns - als riesiger Abfallberg, den wir unseren Kindern und
5 Enkeln hinterlassen.

Mehr als zwei Millionen Tonnen Hausmüll fallen jährlich in Österreich an. Satte 300 Kilogramm pro Kopf. Auch viele Stoffe, die wiederverwertbar wären, landen auf einer der vielen Deponien in unserem Land oder werden verbrannt, was wiederum die Luft verpestet.

Altglas etwa könnte zu 100 Prozent wieder in der Glasproduktion eingesetzt werden. Für die
10 Erzeugung von Glas aus Quarzsand wird viel mehr Energie und auch Wasser verbraucht als beim Einschmelzen der Scherben. Immerhin wird die Hälfte der Einwegflaschen und -gläser schon gesammelt - die andere Hälfte findet man immer noch im Hausmüll.

Plastik ist besonders dauerhaft - vor allem auf den Deponien. Ein echtes Recycling-System gibt es nicht, weil viel zu viele Kunststoffsorten auf dem Markt sind, die der Konsument gar nicht
15 unterscheiden kann. Leider ist der Kunststoffverbrauch in unserem Land in den vergangenen Jahren stark angestiegen - trotz der Warnungen vieler Umweltschützer. (Allein bei den Getränken betrug der Anteil der *Mehrweg*-Glasflaschen 1987 noch 70 Prozent, 1990 aber kaum 40 Prozent. Die fehlenden 30 Prozent hat die PET-Flasche übernommen, die wegen ihrer Größe und Unverrottbarkeit ein wahres Müll-Monster ist.) Die Plastikflut kann eigentlich nur der Konsument
20 stoppen, indem er plastikverpackte Waren gar nicht kauft. Denn auch die biologisch abbaubaren Kunststoffe sind keine Lösung - sie verrotten zwar irgendwann auf natürlichem Weg, belasten aber viele, viele Jahre unsere Deponien.

Eine andere Umwelt*bombe* sind die Getränkedosen aus Aluminium. Sie sind zwar wiederverwert-bar, allerdings wird für die Herstellung und Verarbeitung von Aluminium so viel Energie und
25 Wasser benötigt, daß sogar neue Dosen aus Altmaterial die Umwelt mehr belasten als Mehrweg-Glasflaschen. Deshalb sollte man - auch wenn sie so praktisch und leicht sind - auf die Aludosen verzichten.

Die Müllberge wachsen in den Himmel. In etwa zehn Jahren werden die Gruben, die wir heute für die Lagerung unserer "Wohlstandsreste" verwenden, voll sein. Und was dann?
30 Wir Konsumenten haben es in der Hand, die Wirtschaft zur Erzeugung umweltfreundlicher Produkte und zur Vermeidung von Abfall zu zwingen. So wurde beispielsweise das Verbot der FCKW-Treibgase in Spraydosen unter dem Druck *der Öffentlichkeit* durchgesetzt. Warum sollte dieser Druck nicht auch in anderen Bereichen erfolgreich sein?

(i) Beantworten Sie folgende Fragen – möglichst mit eigenen Worten!

1 Worauf sollten die Leute beim Einkaufen besser achten?

.... (1)

2 Was geschieht mit einem Großteil des Mülls, und was ist das Problem dabei?

....

.... (2)

3 Wieviel Abfall wirft jeder Österreicher im Durchschnitt jährlich weg?

.... (1)

4 Warum ist das Verbrennen von Müll keine gute Lösung?

.... (1)

5 Was sind die Vorteile von Altglas in der Glasproduktion?

....

.... (2)

6 Warum können zur Zeit nur 50% der Glasbehälter wiederverwertet werden?

....

.... (2)

7 Was sind die Probleme bei der Wiederverwertung von Kunststoffen?

....

.... (2)

8 Welche negative Entwicklung hat es in den letzten Jahren bei den Getränkeflaschen gegeben?

....

.... (2)

9 Was sind die Vor- und Nachteile der Aluminiumdosen im Vergleich zu Glasflaschen?

....

....

.... (3)

10 Wie können die Konsumenten die Situation ändern?

....

.... (2)

11 Warum ist der Journalist optimistisch, daß die Konsumenten etwas ändern können?

....

.... (2)

(ii) Im Text finden Sie die folgenden Satzteile. Erklären Sie die kursivgedruckten Wörter/Wortteile auf deutsch:

1 *Mehrweg*-Glasflaschen (Zeile 17)

.... (2)

2 Umwelt*bombe* (Zeile 23)

.... (2)

3 unter dem Druck *der Öffentlichkeit*

.... (2)

There is another exercise set on this text in the Writing unit, Task A.

NEAB

Read this passage and answer in German the questions which follow it.

Rio – Weltkonferenz: Umwelt und Entwicklung
Ein ZEIT-Gespräch mit Umweltminister Klaus Töpfer

ZEIT: Herr Minister, wird die Bundesregierung das *Tempolimit* auf Autobahnen einführen?
Töpfer: Sicherlich brauchen wir verstärkt Geschwindigkeitsbegrenzungen, um die Verkehrssicherheit zu erhöhen, den Verkehrsfluß zu verbessern und um die Umweltbelastungen zu verringern.

5 **ZEIT:** Beim Erdgipfel in Rio de Janeiro haben Sie mit dem Versprechen viel Lob geerntet, den Ausstoß des klimaschädlichen Kohlendioxids bis zum Jahr 2005 um mindestens ein Viertel zu verringern. Wie wollen sie Ihr Wort halten?
Töpfer: Wir sind in Rio ernst genommen worden, weil wir nicht nur ein Ziel, sondern auch einen klaren Maßnahmenkatalog mitgebracht haben. Allein der energiepolitische Umbau in den neuen
10 Bundesländern wird die CO_2-Emissionen massiv verringern. Außerdem werden bessere Kraftwerke große Entlastungen bringen. Hier *geht es* doch nur *darum*, ob diese neuen Kraftwerke bis zum Jahr 2005 wirklich am Netz sind.

Die eine offene Frage ist tatsächlich die Verkehrspolitik - nicht etwa, weil beim Autoverkehr große Chancen für eine CO_2-Minderung sind, sondern weil ich dort auf jeden Fall eine
15 Stabilisierung erreichen muß. Wenn das nicht *klappt*, wird es wirklich schwierig, das Gesamtziel zu erreichen. Deshalb müssen wir noch in den nächsten zwei Jahren die Bundesbahn so stärken, daß sie endlich das tun kann, was wir in Sonntagsreden dauernd fordern: Mehr Menschen und mehr Güter *auf die Schiene locken.*
ZEIT: In den neuen Bundesländern geschieht zur Zeit genau das Gegenteil: Alles drängt von der
20 Schiene auf die Straße. Diese nachholende Entwicklung ist doch wohl kaum mit der in Rio vereinbarten „nachhaltigen Entwicklung" in Einklang zu bringen.
Töpfer: In den alten Bundesländern teilen sich zwei Menschen ein Auto, in den neuen Ländern waren es vier. Es findet dort ein Aufholprozeß statt, der aber keine langfristige Perspektive darstellt - das kann nur unser geändertes Verhalten sein.
25 Ich kann mir durchaus vorstellen, daß wir zum nächsten Gipfeltreffen nicht mehr mit dem Flugzeug anreisen, sondern daß wir per Bildschirm zusammengebracht werden. Von solchen Veränderungen unseres Alltags hat beispielsweise der amerikanische Präsident in Rio leider nicht geredet. Sein Votum war schlicht: Durch Wachstum die Umweltprobleme abbauen. Das halte ich, gelinde gesagt, für eine sehr vereinfachende Aussage. Entscheidend ist die Veränderung von
30 menschlichem Verhalten in den Industriestaaten.

(Die Zeit)

(i) Beantworten Sie folgende Fragen – möglichst mit eigenen Worten!

1 Was sind laut Töpfer die drei Vorteile, die Geschwindigkeitsbegrenzungen mit sich bringen?

....

....

.... (3)

2 Was hat Töpfer in Rio versprochen?

....

.... (2)

3 Was brauchte man außer einem klaren Ziel, um in Rio ernst genommen zu werden?

.... (1)

4 Was muß vor allem geschehen, damit die CO_2-Emissionen in den neuen Bundesländern verringert werden?

....

.... (2)

5 In welchem Fall wird es schwierig sein, das Gesamtziel zu erreichen?

....

.... (2)

6 Geben Sie das Beispiel für die „nachholende Entwicklung" in den neuen Bundesländern!

....

.... (2)

7 Was ist für Töpfer entscheidend für den Abbau der Umweltprobleme?

....

.... (2)

(ii) Im Text finden Sie die folgenden Ausdrücke. Wie hätte man die kursivgedruckten Wörter auf deutsch anders formulieren können?

1 das *Tempolimit* auf Autobahnen einführen (Zeile 1)

.... (1)

2 Hier *geht es* doch nur *darum* (Zeile 11)

.... (1)

3 Wenn das nicht *klappt* (Zeile 15)

.... (1)

4 *auf die Schiene locken* (Zeile 18)

.... (2)

NEAB

TASK K

Refer back to the text accompanying Task J. Do the following translation as a starter. It should be easier now that you (hopefully!) understand the context provided by the whole of the text.

Übersetzen Sie Zeilen 22–28 (*In den alten … nicht geredet*) ins Englische!

TASK L

Refer back to the text accompanying Task E. Translate into English the last two paragraphs.

TASK M

Refer back to the text accompanying Task G. Translate into English the last two paragraphs.

TASK N

Translate the following passage into English.

Tätigkeiten im Haushalt bleiben in Familien mit Kindern und erwerbstätigen Müttern weiterhin den Frauen überlassen. Eine gleichmäßige und partnerschaftliche Arbeitsteilung in Doppelverdiensthaushalten mit Kindern scheitert offenbar weiterhin an der fehlenden Bereitschaft der Männer, ihren Frauen im Haushalt einen wesentlichen Teil der Arbeit abzunehmen.

Familienväter sind am Tag rund zwei Stunden mit häuslichen Arbeiten, wie Reparaturen, Gartenarbeit und Fahrzeugpflege beschäftigt. Im traditionell weiblichen Arbeitsbereich beteiligen sie sich lediglich am Einkaufen und an der Kinderbetreuung.

Die tägliche Routinearbeit im Haushalt – Kochen, Spülen, Putzen und Wäschepflege – bleibt jedoch weitgehend den Müttern und Frauen überlassen. Die tägliche Hausarbeitszeit erwerbstätiger Mütter errechneten die Statistiker mit durchschnittlich fünf bis sechs Stunden.

[15]
Die Welt

NICCEA

TASK 0

Background Information

You are working on the topic *Die neuen Bundesländer*. For this you are required to summarise the following passage about the birth rate in Saxony.

Instructions

Write the summary required for your study. Your summary must be written **in English** and should contain between 190 and 210 words. Do not write more than 210 words, as no credit will be given for additional material. You must write in continuous prose, not note form. State the number of words you have used; there are 408 words in the original. [30]

Geburtenrückgang in Sachsen

DRESDEN – Wird Sachsen ein kinderloses Land? Auf dem Gebiet des bevölkerungsreichsten der östlichen Länder kamen 1980 immerhin 71 000 Babys zur Welt - 1992 waren es nur noch 25 000. Ministerpräsident Kurt Biedenkopf warnte: „Daß wir uns mitten in einer demographischen Revolution befinden, ist unserer Bevölkerung nicht bewußt.“ Noch habe man die Wahl, sich darauf einzustellen, alles treiben zu lassen, junge Menschen aus dem Ausland einwandern zu lassen oder Anreize für Schwangerschaften zu geben. Bleibe alles beim alten, steige bis zum Jahr 2030 der Anteil der über 60jährigen von heute einem Fünftel auf ein Drittel der Bevölkerung.

Während im Westen die Geburenrate etwa gleichbleibt, geht sie in den neuen Ländern weiter steil nach unten. Noch 1989 kamen im Westen elf, in der DDR immerhin zwölf Säuglinge auf 1000 Einwohner. Bis heute bleibt die Zahl in den alten Ländern stabil, im Osten aber sank sie von 11,1 (1990) über 6,8 (1991) auf nur noch 5,5 im vorigen Jahr. Diese Zahlen nennt der sächsische Sozialminister Hans Geisler „beunruhigend“.

Noch fehlen verläßliche Analysen über die Ursachen, auch sind regionale Unterschiede erst oberflächlich erfaßt worden. Hebammen haben vor allem dort seit 1989 wesentlich weniger zu tun, wo die Aussichten auf den Aufschwung klein, die Arbeitslosigkeit und die Abwanderung in den Westen aber groß sind.

Außerdem wirkt sich nun die Familienpolitik der SED aus. Als Anfang der siebziger Jahre in der DDR Abtreibungen erlaubt und neue Verhütungsmittel eingeführt wurden, gab es hier den „Pillenknick“, den die Westdeutschen schon fünf Jahre eher erlebt hatten. Heute fehlen die jungen Mütter dieser Jahrgänge.

Geislers Fachleute haben jüngst eine ernüchternde Analyse vorgestellt: Die Delle im „Lebensbaum“ und auch der Wegzug junger Eltern in den Westen sind zwar mit schuld am Rückgang der Geburtenzahl, aber zu zwei Dritteln handele es sich um „subjektive Faktoren“, sagt der Minister. „Die Menschen spüren die wirtschaftliche Krise, verzichten auf Kinder oder verschieben den Wunsch auf Nachwuchs.“

Geisler äußert sich wenig optimistisch. Es gebe eine „Schallgrenze, bis zu der wir mit finanziellen Anreizen etwas bewegen können“. Weil diese noch nicht erreicht ist, streitet Geisler für die Erhöhung der Steuerfreibetragsgrenze und Hilfen für Mütter. Ihnen solle mit Lohnzuschüssen der Wiedereinstieg in den Beruf erleichtert werden, außerdem dürften zumindest im öffentlichen Dienst die Karrierewege trotz Schwangerschaftspause nicht verbaut werden. Schließlich denkt Geisler auch an moralische Appelle: „Kindergeschrei stört nicht nur, es ist auch ein Zeichen für Leben.“ Er prangert die „individualistische Gesellschaft“ an: in ihr würden Kinder gemieden, folglich sei sie in jeder Hinsicht unfruchtbar.

Hannoversche Allgemeine Zeitung
21.10.93

Oxford and Cambridge

Summarise in English the information given in the following article about a report by the German Education Minister, which was adopted by the German Cabinet, on training for work in Eastern Germany. Do not summarise the introductory paragraph, but you may include the title and sub-title. Try to make 20 separate points in no more than 230 words.

Kein neues Lehrstellenprogramm für den Osten

Der Bildungsminister setzt lieber auf Zusagen der Wirtschaft, mehr Plätze anzubieten

hmu **Bonn** (Eigener Bericht) – *Zur Bekämpfung der Lehrstellenprobleme in den neuen Bundesländern soll es in diesem Jahr keine neue Gemeinschaftsinitiative Ost geben. Das sagte Bundesbildungsminister Jürgen Rüttgers (CDU) bei der Vorstellung des vom Kabinett verabschiedeten „Perspektivberichts Berufliche Bildung". Er setze voll auf die Lehrstellenzusage der Wirtschaft, erklärte Rüttgers.*

Die Wirtschaft habe zugesagt, bis 1997 die Zahl der Ausbildungsplätze um zehn Prozent anzuheben, mit einer überproportionalen Steigerung in den neuen Ländern. Bisher habe sie die Lehrstellenzahl um rund zwei Prozent gesteigert. „Das heißt, daß ein Zuwachs von weiteren acht Prozent aussteht", mahnte der Minister. Nach seiner Darstellung werden im Osten Deutschlands 1996 und 1997 jeweils 140 000 Ausbildungsplätze benötigt, rund 12 000 mehr als im vergangenen Jahr. 65 Prozent der Lehrstellen im Osten werden inzwischen von Bund, Ländern und der Bundesanstalt für Arbeit subventioniert. Mit der Gemeinschaftsinitiative haben Bund und Länder im vergangenen Jahr 14 500 zusätzliche außerbetriebliche Lehrstellen finanziert. Davon sind 1700 Plätze nach Angaben Rüttgers bis heute nicht besetzt. Die Kosten für die Gemeinschaftsinitiative bezifferte er auf 860 Millionen DM, von denen der Bund die Hälfte getragen habe.

Für den Westen Deutschlands sind nach Berechnung der Bundesregierung 1996 rund 480 000 und 1997 über 490 000 Ausbildungsplätze erforderlich; 1995 waren es 470 000. Bonn werde seinen Beitrag zur Ausbildungsplatzsicherung auch in diesem Jahr leisten, versprach Rüttgers. So soll es in der Bundesverwaltung 1996 mindestens fünf Prozent mehr Lehrstellen geben.

Der Bundesbildungsminister sieht jetzt vor allem die Länder und Kommunen in der Pflicht. Sie hätten sich bisher geweigert, konkrete Zahlen vorzulegen, kritisierte Rüttgers. Doch nur so sei die Vermutung aus der Welt zu schaffen, daß sich die Länder und Kommunen aus ihrer Ausbildungsverantwortung gegenüber den jungen Menschen zurückzögen.

Nach Angaben Rüttgers bilden heute nur ein Drittel der Unternehmen Lehrlinge aus. Deshalb will die Bundesregierung durch einen mit Wirtschaft und Gewerkschaft abgestimmten Maßnahmenkatalog die Ausbildungsbereitschaft besonders kleinerer Betriebe stärken. Danach sollen die Länder den Berufsschulunterricht flexibler organisieren. Ein schulisches Berufsbildungsjahr vor der Lehre soll in Zukunft nur noch mit sechs Monaten bei der Ausbildungszeit angerechnet werden. Wer älter als 18 ist, soll an Berufsschultagen wieder zurück in den Betrieb.

Süddeutsche Zeitung 29 Feb 1996

4 *Writing*

REVISION
SUMMARY

ASSESSMENT OBJECTIVES

This unit shows you how to tackle the different examination tasks which are set specifically to test your ability to write in fluent and correct German as opposed to testing your ability to show comprehension.

Depending on your syllabus, these may include:

● explaining an English stimulus in German;

● translating an English text into German;

● writing compositions on general topics from 100–120 to 400–500 words in length;

● literature and 'civilisation' essays.

There are examples in this unit of all these types of Writing task with some Examiner's tips.

It is a good idea to attempt to answer the specimen tasks yourself before reading the specimen answer and the accompanying Examiner's tip.

EXAMINATION TECHNIQUE

The technique varies according to the task. Specific advice on all these tasks including essay writing is given with the relevant specimen questions and answers.

    A general comment only is needed here. The accuracy of your German is more important here than for any other skill or assessment objective. It is not specifically tested in Reading and Listening. In Speaking more tolerance is made of errors, partly because they are more natural in speech even in one's own native tongue, and partly because it is particularly difficult for a non-native speaker not to make mistakes in spoken German with its complex system of case endings and word order. However, you have time in writing to think and also to check your work. You will be expected to show a high degree of accuracy, if you are aiming at the top grade. As with Speaking, your range of expression and natural idiom will also be assessed. You must try to develop a broad variety of structures, without sacrificing your accuracy.

WHAT TO REVISE FOR WRITING

To tackle all the tasks in this unit you need to bear in mind some essential points of German grammar. Here is a checklist to help you revise before the examination and also to enable you to correct your mistakes when re-reading your work in the examination room – always leave plenty of time for this!

Grammar checklist

The references in brackets [ ] are to examples in the tasks, e.g. [Task C6/8] means Task C points 6 and 8. Sometimes the reference is to a sentence of the specimen answer. Refer to these for more information.

❶ **Nouns**

    Correct gender? Is gender consistent throughout my answers? Plural spelling [C3]? Dative -*n*?

❷ **Adjectives**

    ● Endings: If not followed by a noun, no ending needed. If placed before a noun (and also when used as a noun) it must have an ending which depends on gender and case of noun [B1/E5]. Do I know the three categories of endings?

- Comparative/Superlative: The forms and comparative expressions. Am I familiar with these [B17]?

❸ Cases

- Can I list the different case endings of articles, pronouns, possessive (e.g. *mein*) and demonstrative (e.g. *dieser*) adjectives?

- What case comes after the verb? Do I know verbs which are **not** followed by the usual accusative? **Nominative**: *bleiben, sein, werden, scheinen, heißen* (when it means 'to be called'), *nennen* (when used in the passive), *sich fühlen als* being the most common. **Dative**: a fair list – have I learnt the most common [C9]?

- Have I met the most common adjectives followed by the dative (e.g. *dankbar*) or genitive (e.g. *bewußt*) without a preposition?

❹ Preposition and cases

- Which take accusative? genitive [D14/E17]? dative [B18]? accusative or dative depending on meaning (position/motion) [C2/E6]?

- Some adjectives are also followed by prepositions (e.g. *böse auf* + accusative)[B4/B16].

- Which case for expressions of definite time, duration of time, quantities and measurements, direction up or down *den Berg hinauf*? – **Accusative**!

- Which case for expressions of indefinite time? – **Genitive**!

❺ Verbs

- Agreement: Does the verb agree with the subject of my sentence [C6/D12/E9]?

- Tense: Do I know which tense to use [B11/B19]? Is my formation of each tense sound?

- Auxiliary verbs: Right auxiliary – *haben* or *sein* [B5]? *sein* – intransitive verbs: verbs showing change of place (from A to B) or change of state (e.g. *aufwachen*), verbs meaning 'to happen', 'to fail', 'to succeed', + *begegnen, bleiben, sein, werden.*

- Table: Have I remembered my table of strong and mixed verbs?

- Modal verbs: Can I use modal verbs correctly [B10/E15]?

- Separable verbs: Do I know which verbs are separable or inseparable [C5/10]?

❻ Word order

- Does my verb come as the second idea in the main clause [C8/E11]? If it's a question without an interrogative word, the verb starts the sentence: *Kommst du morgen*? If a subordinate clause precedes it, the verb comes first in the main clause [C7].

- Do I know which (co-ordinating) conjunctions do not affect the word order [B7]?

- Have I put the verb at the end of the subordinate clause after subordinating conjunctions [B9/B10/E7]? and in infinitive phrases?

- What about time, reason, manner, place in that order: *Ich bin gestern wegen des schönen Wetters schnell zum Strand gefahren* [B2/D2]?

- And those tricky rules about the order of objects: pronoun before noun (*Ich gab es dem Mann*), accusative pronoun before a dative one (*Ich gab es ihm*), other way round with nouns – dative before accusative (*Ich gab dem Mann das Buch*).

- Where on earth do I put *nicht*? Before a predicative noun or adjective, an infinitive, past participle, separable prefix, adverb or adverbial phrase of manner or degree (or, if these are not present, of place). In a subordinate clause with only subject and verb, *nicht* obviously comes before the finite verb: *Weil Cantona nicht spielt.*

- And where does the reflexive pronoun *sich* go [D13]?

❼ Subjunctive

Do I know how the subjunctive is formed and used? In reported speech, indirect questions [B15], in clauses with *wenn* meaning 'if' and a past tense and in conditional statements [C4/C7/D5], in *als ob* or *als wenn* clauses, with modal verbs to mean what ought to have happened or what might happen.

Have I used the correct tense of the subjunctive [B8]?

❽ Passive

Can I avoid the passive with *man* or a reflexive verb? [Tasks I and J in the Reading unit]. Can I use *man* correctly when I am talking about people in a general sense, or do I wrongly use other pronouns like *er, du, sie, wir* or even a mixture of these.

❾ Spelling

Capital letter on nouns? Umlaut needed or not needed [B19/C3/C4/D4]? Confusion of *ß* and *ss* [E8], of relative pronoun *das* and conjunction *daß*, of *ie* and *ei*. Have I put *ch* where I needed *sch*?

❿ Punctuation

The comma is most tricky. Where do I put it?

- between two main clauses linked by a co-ordinating conjunction;
- before a subordinate clause;
- in lists (but **not** before *und*).

SAMPLE QUESTIONS AND ANSWERS

Translation into German

This task is based upon the text accompanying Task I in the Reading unit. Ideally, you should have completed that task before you tackle this one, because it will help you with vocabulary.

Übersetzen Sie ins Deutsche:

Although environmentalists are forever warning us that our rubbish tips will be full by the end of this century, most people still buy their drinks in plastic bottles or aluminium cans. We use up large amounts of energy in their production, and then they never decompose. But people must change their shopping habits today in order to save the world for their grandchildren. If they bought only products in environmentally friendly packaging, industry would react quickly to such consumer pressure.

Obwohl uns <u>Umweltschützer</u> immer davor warnen, daß unsere <u>Deponien</u> bis zum Ende des Jahrhunderts <u>voll sein</u> werden, kaufen die meisten Leute ihre <u>Getränke</u> in <u>Plastikflaschen</u> oder in <u>Aluminiumdosen</u>. Wir <u>verbrauchen</u> sehr viel/eine Menge <u>Energie</u> bei ihrer <u>Herstellung</u>, und dann <u>verrotten</u> sie nie. Aber <u>Konsumenten</u> müssen heute ihre <u>Einkaufsgewohnheiten</u> (ver)<u>ändern</u>, um die Welt für ihre <u>Enkel</u>(kinder) zu retten. Wenn sie nur Produkte kaufen würden/kauften, die <u>umweltfreundlich verpackt</u> sind, würde die Industrie auf einen solchen Konsumentendruck/<u>Druck</u> von <u>Konsumenten</u> schnell reagieren.

> **Examiner's commentary** You are not being asked to remember a lot of specialist vocabulary in an active sense. Provided your passive vocabulary – your ability to recognise the English meaning of German words – is of a high standard, you should have a head start here. All the words underlined in the answer are to be found somewhere in the text for Task I in the Reading unit. Although the verb *warnen* is not in the passage, the noun *Warnungen* is there to help you. You could get away with adapting the passage only slightly for the first sentence of your answer by writing: *Trotz ständiger Warnungen von Umweltschützern, daß ...* The skill is to re-read the passage after reading the text you have to translate, in order to spot the required vocabulary. If you can bear the translation into German in mind, whilst you are doing the comprehension questions (in Parts (i) and (ii) of the Task I in the Reading unit), it will save time when you come to put these ideas into German. Apart from your ability to notice and re-use words (which was also necessary for paraphrasing in the Reading comprehension task), your knowledge of grammar and sentence structure is being tested. Check your answer thoroughly for accuracy upon completion.

Translate the following passage into German.

It was Andrea Pfeiffer's first visit to Britain. And because she lived in a small town in Lower Saxony she had to fly to England from Hanover via Cologne, which was particularly awkward, as she had to spend three hours there waiting for her plane. She had never flown before but she wasn't afraid. In fact she was more angry than anything, because her mother had insisted that she take far more than she needed for a 14-day stay, and so she had a very heavy suitcase, though she would probably have to carry it only a fairly short distance herself.

Caroline and her family were going to meet her at the airport and take her home. She wondered what sort of car they had. Her father had had a Nissan for years and she hoped the Browns would have a proper English car. But when they did finally meet they went home by taxi, because Caroline's father needed the car for business that day. Caroline's mum was terribly nice, even though she kept asking questions. Would she like a sandwich? Did she drink tea? Did she feel tired after the journey?

The best thing about Caroline's house was that it was nice and old with spacious rooms and a big back garden where she could play with Caroline's younger brother and the dog. This, she thought, was going to be a very pleasant exchange. Why had she been so worried beforehand?

Oxford and Cambridge

ANSWER

This contains errors, as indicated by the numbers. As you read it through, try to correct the errors yourself. Then read the Examiner's commentary.

Es war Andrea Pfeiffers erste[1] Besuch in Großbritannien, und weil sie in einer kleinen Stadt in Niedersachsen wohnte, mußte sie nach England fliegen, von Hannover über Köln[2], das[3] besonders umständlich war, da sie drei Stunden in Köln verbringen mußte, indem sie für[4] ihre Maschine wartete. Sie hatte[5] nie zuvor geflogen, aber sie fürchtete sich nicht. In der Tat war sie eher verärgert als alles[6], denn ihre Mutter darauf bestanden hatte[7], daß sie bei weitem mehr Kleidung mitnahme[8], als sie benötigte für einen 14-tägigen Aufenthalt[9], also hatte sie einen sehr schweren Koffer, obwohl sie ihn selbst wahrscheinlich nur eine kürzere Strecke tragen müssen würde[10].

Caroline und ihre Familie trafen[11] sie am Flughafen und brachten[11] sie nach Hause. Sie fragte sich, was für einen Wagen sie wohl hätten. Ihr Vater hatte schon seit Jahren einen Nissan und sie hoffte, die Familie Browns[12] würde einen richtigen englischen Wagen haben. Aber als sie sich schließlich trafen, fuhren sie mit einem Taxi nach Hause, weil Carolines Vater an diesem Tag den Wagen für Geschäft[13] brauchte. Carolines Mutti war furchtbar sympathisch, selbst wenn sie nicht aufhörte, Fragen über Fragen zu stellen[14]. Ob sie ein belegtes Brot möchte. Ob sie Tee trinke. Ob sie sich nach der Reise müde fühle[15].

Das Beste über[16] Carolines Haus war, daß es schön alt war mit geräumigen Zimmern und einem großen Hintergarten, wo sie mit Carolines jungerem[17] Bruder und der[18] Hund spielen konnte[19]. Dies, sie dachte[20], würde ein sehr angenehmer Austausch sein. Warum hatte sie sich vorher solche Sorgen gemacht?

the imperfect subjunctive is the same as the imperfect indicative, e.g. *machte*, even conversationally you should use the present tense, e.g. *mache*, to show subjunctive. Similarly, where the correct literary tense would be the same as the indicative in spelling – this applies to **all** tenses – e.g. *sie kommen/sie machen*, you must use the conversational tense, e.g. *sie kämen/sie machten*, even though for weak verbs like *sie machten* the imperfect indicative and subjunctive are identical. You could use a modal verb: *mitnehmen sollte/mußte*.

9 The dangers of a word for word translation! The verb *benötigte* should come at the end of the clause.

10 When you use a modal verb (*dürfen, können, mögen, müssen, sollen, wollen*) in a compound tense (future or conditional, perfect or pluperfect) in a subordinate clause with a dependent infinitive, you must put the auxiliary of the compound tense (*werden/sein/haben*) before the dependent infinitive and **not** at the end of the clause. Write here: *würde tragen müssen*. Similarly: *weil ich diese Kleider habe/hatte tragen müssen*.

11 The imperfect *trafen* means 'met' or 'were meeting'; similar mistake with *brachten*. The conditional is needed to render 'were going to meet/take' (or 'would meet/take'): *würden … treffen/bringen*. Alternatively, use a modal: *wollten/sollten … treffen/bringen*.

12 Correct possibilities in German are: *Browns, die Browns, die Familie Brown*.

13 Another literal translation! Use *geschäftlich*.

14 A nice turn of phrase (note position of *nicht*). You could also put: *auch wenn sie unaufhörlich/immer wieder Fragen stellte*.

15 Notice the use of subjunctive for an indirect question after *ob*. In this elliptical use of *ob*, the idea of *sie fragte* is understood without being stated. Later, there is another indirect question: *Sie fragte sich, was für einen Wagen sie wohl hätten*.

16 Correct preposition is *an* (+ dative).

17 The comparative has an Umlaut: *jüngerem*. Learn the list of monosyllabic adjectives which follow this pattern; some are easily learnt in pairs: *alt – jung, lang – kurz, stark – schwach, klug – dumm, warm – kalt, krank – gesund* (except that *gesund* is sometimes used in the comparative without Umlaut). Do you know any others where an Umlaut is a) optional b) necessary?

18 This is still dependent on the preposition *mit*, so dative: *dem Hund*.

19 English speakers muddle up *konnte* and *könnte*, because they can both be translated as 'could': *konnte* (imperfect indicative) means that during her stay she was able to play. Her stay has only just begun; she is imagining that she might be able to play, so: *könnte* (imperfect subjunctive).

20 This is not the start of the sentence, but a remark in parenthesis, here after *Dies*, so inversion is needed: *dachte sie*.

Mini-essays of 100–120 words

The following task is based upon the text accompanying Task H in the Reading unit. Ideally, you should have completed that task before you tackle this one, since the German text will give you a few ideas as well as some indication of how to express them in German.

*Geben Sie Ihre Ansicht zum Thema Vaterrechte. Schreiben Sie bis zu 120 Wörtern auf **deutsch** dazu.*

Cambridge

TASK C

ANSWER

Meiner Ansicht nach ergibt[1] das Problem daraus, daß wir Gesetze suchen, die schwarz auf weiß sind und in alle Fälle[2] gelten. Wir sollten bereit sein, jeden Fall unterschiedlich zu betrachten. Bei Streitfallen[3] muß man sich in beiden[2] Rollen versetzen, das heißt das Problem aus zwei Perspektiven sehen. So mußte[4] der Vater sicherstellen, daß sowohl sein Kind als auch seine Frau von ihm ausreichend finanziell untergestützt[5] würde[6]. Erst wenn er das leistet, er bekäme[7] das Recht, Kontakt zu seinem Kind zu haben. Anderseits man muß[8] auch die Mutter verstehen, die nicht will, daß das Kind von einem getrennten Ehepartner beeinflußt wird. Die Mütter[3] kann befürchten, daß das Kind mehr Gefühle für den Vater empfindet und sich später ganz zum Vater bekennt. Darin besteht aber kein echter Grund, den[9] Vater seine Rechte zu vorenthalten[10].

Examiner's commentary   A mature approach to the question which impresses by trying to see both sides. Try not to be too opinionated and dogmatic or simplistic. There are some good vocabulary items and structures here, and the writing is fairly accurate. There are 132 words; try not to write more than 10 or so over the stipulated limit, otherwise the excess may well not be marked.

1 *sich* should be inserted here. There are many reflexive verbs in German. Make a point of learning some, but revise the position of the reflexive pronoun *sich*.

2 *in allen Fällen* dative; later accusative needed with *sich versetzen*: *in beide Rollen*. Revise the use of these cases with prepositions.

3 Plural slip – *Fälle* with Umlaut, as used earlier. Later an Umlaut is added to create a plural *Mütter* when singular is intended. Be careful with singular and plural forms. Too many candidates lose valuable marks by ignoring their significance.

4 A common error: here the missing Umlaut changes the tense/mood: *mußte* = had to (imperfect indicative). You need *müßte* = would have to (imperfect subjunctive).

5 Learn separable and inseparable verbs: *unterstützen* is inseparable, so there is no *ge-* in the past participle – *unterstützt*. See note **10**.

6 It's very easy in a subordinate clause, when the subject is separated from the verb by a line or two, to forget to make them agree. *Sowohl ... als auch* is followed by a plural verb form: *würden*, even though both subjects are singular!

7 Word order slip – inversion needed: after a subordinate clause the main clause will start with the verb – *bekäme er ...* Notice good use of the subjunctive following the *wenn* clause.

8 Inversion again. Verb must come as second idea in the main clause: *muß man ...*

9 Dative of person with this verb: *einem* (dative) *etwas* (accusative) *vorenthalten*, so: *dem Vater ...*

10 As the verb is separable, *zu* comes in between the separable prefix *vor* and the verb *enthalten*: *vorzuenthalten*.

Longer general essays

By general essays we mean compositions which are not set specifically to test your ability to appreciate literature or to understand areas of civilisation detailed in the syllabus for special study.

Their purpose is to see if you can express your own ideas in good, fluent German on aspects of everyday life. There are various types:

❶ Discursive essays, where you are given a statement or a theme and are invited to discuss it.

❷ Creative essays, where you may tell a story or continue one suggested.

❸ Essays based on a stimulus which could be visual, a written German text, or an audio or video tape recording of German.

❹ Newspaper or magazine articles.

5 Letters.

6 Dialogues or monologues: you invent a conversation (possibly even on the telephone) or a script for a debate or for a radio or television broadcast.

Before we look at a specimen task and answer, let us consider what our approach to this type of writing should be. This series of hints may help.

- Avoid the temptation to write a pre-learnt composition. Try to target what you have previously learnt about a topic to the actual question set. The wording of the question is crucial, because it shows what aspects you have to deal with.

- Plan what you are going to write. A plan is **not** a random series of notes. Try to group your ideas under headings and put everything into a logical order. A plan will also help you to keep to time and finish your work properly.

- Do not leap into the first sentence with your categorical answer to the question or problem being debated (essay types 1/3/4/5/6 are prone to this). Develop your argument steadily.

- Don't generalise about the subject; be specific to the question.

- Try not to go off at tangents, for you soon become irrelevant. Stick to the point.

- Adhere to a clear structure with paragraphs/individual speeches in dialogues of sensible length. Marks will usually be awarded for organisation of the composition.

- Make sure you have a conclusion in which your story/conversation/composition has a clear ending and in which your own views are made clear (essay types 1/3/4/5) without tedious repetition of previous points.

- Check your language for accuracy against the checklist given at the beginning of this chapter. Remember that marks awarded for language are likely to be a substantial proportion of the total.

A profile of candidate performance on the A-level German examination as a whole shows the composition to be the weakest area. It is the biggest hurdle for those wishing to gain the top grades, particularly an A.

Before you attempt some tasks on your own, here is a specimen question and answer to prepare the ground.

TASK D

„Das Leben fängt mit 70 an!“

Stellen Sie sich vor, Sie erreichen das Alter von 70. Wie wird das Leben für Sie 'anfangen' ?

Cambridge

So far we have used simulated candidate answers to illustrate good and bad points. We now print an actual answer, of a high standard, from an examination paper. Read it through once without looking at the Examiner's tips and note the good points. You may also notice some errors. Then read the advice which follows the essay.

ANSWER

Wegen der steigenden Lebenserwartung ist das Thema von alten Leuten oft erörtert. Ich könnte selbst bis über neunzig leben und deshalb will ich mich hier bemühen zu diskutieren, warum ich hoffentlich ganz positiv das Leben „anfangen“ würde aber auch die negative Seite des Alters.

Ich möchte mit der positiven Seite beginnen, weil die vorwiegend negative Beschreibung des letzten Lebensabschnitts allen älteren Leuten nicht zutritt[1] und persönlich hoffe ich in den Ruhestand ganz entspannt[2] zu treten. Ich werde vom Streß der Arbeitswelt befreit sein und werde deshalb die Zeit zur Verfügung haben, um das Leben endlich zu „genießen“. Ich könnte neue Hobbys anfangen oder alten Interessen nachgehen und hoffentlich werden dabei neue Bekanntschaften entstehen. Ich könnte etwas machen, was ich nie die Zeit dazu[3] finden könnte[4], zum Beispiel reisen oder sogar auswandern! Obwohl ich nicht mehr berufstätig wäre, brauche[5] ich nicht arbeitslos[6] zu sein, da ich an mehr Aktivitäten in der Gesellschaft teilnehmen könnte, zum Beispiel freiwillige Arbeit, was sehr befriedigend sein kann.

Die Verantwortlichkeit der[7] Familie wäre einigermaßen vorbei und am Besten würde ich Enkelkinder haben und könnte Freude daran nehmen[8], sie aufwachsen zu sehen.

Andererseits könnte ich auch unter Problemen leiden. Auch mit der Ausweitung sozialpolitischer Leistungen könnte ich finanzielle Probleme haben, insbesondere wegen der Veralterung der Gesellschaft, da der Staat vielleicht verpflichtet würde[9], weniger Renten zu bezahlen. Mein Gesundheitsstand[10] könnte auch eine Sorge sein. Physikalische Probleme sind frustrierend, zum Beispiel, was nutzt es, wenn ich mehr Zeit habe, um mein Lieblingshobby, Gärtern[11], zu verfolgen, wenn ich mich nicht bücken kann? Vielleicht werde ich nicht so gut sehen oder hören können und, wenn meine Schwierigkeiten bedeuten, daß ich für mich selbst nicht mehr sorgen kann, muß ich vielleicht entweder bei der Familie oder im Altersheim wohnen. Hier könnte ich fühlen, daß ich eine Belastung sei, und insbesondere im Heim, daß ich meine Selbständigkeit verloren hätte. Auch wenn ich zu Hause wohnen[12], könnte ich[13] isoliert fühlen, insbesondere, wenn ich Witwe wäre, und vielleicht würde ich meinen Ruhestand nicht genießen und in Melancholie verfallen.

Ich muß deshalb zu der Überzeugung kommen, daß sowohl die negative als auch die positive Seite des Alters mein „neues Leben" beeinflüssen könnten. Ich hoffe, vielleicht trotz[14] Probleme wie diejenigen oben erwähnt, meinen Ruhestand zu genießen aber es scheint mir auch, daß, wenn wir, wie in den Entwicklungsländern, Respekt für alte Leute hätten, das Altsein als positiver angesehen würde.

Examiner's commentary There are some inaccuracies, which are mostly minor. There is an excellent range of vocabulary and structures, with good use of word order and subordinate clauses. The hypothetical treatment of the subject enables the candidate to introduce conditional tenses and subjunctives. This is more sophisticated and entertaining than writing with plain statements in the future tense. The required personal viewpoint is put into a sociological and political perspective: the difficulty of financing and caring for the large proportion of old people which our society will contain when the candidate reaches old age.

Some words are repeated for example *insbesondere*, where a synonym would be better: *besonders/vor allem*. Other possible synonyms: *in Pension gehen* for *in den Ruhestand treten; der Lebensabend* for *das Alter.*

Correction of errors:

1 Perhaps the candidate meant *zutrifft* which is used with *auf* or *für* (+ accusative). Or use *betreffen* (+ accusative).

2 Manner before place: *ganz entspannt in den Ruhestand.*

3 *wozu ich nie die Zeit finden …*

4 Imperfect indicative *konnte* (no Umlaut!), referring to one's past life, is needed here, not imperfect subjunctive which is hypothetical.

5 Imperfect subjunctive *brauchte* = would not need.

6 *unbeschäftigt* is meant here.

7 *Die Verantwortlichkeit für die Familie.*

8 Anglicism – use *Freude haben.*

9 *sein* is missing here: *verpflichtet sein würde*, or write: *verpflichtet wäre.*

10 *Gesundheitszustand.*

11 *Gärtnern = im Garten arbeiten/die Gartenarbeit machen.*

12 *wohne* – the only more serious slip in the essay.

13 *mich* is missing: *könnte ich mich isoliert fühlen.*

14 *trotz der Probleme …*

If you wish to try your hand at writing a non-literary essay, turn to the Exam Practice at the end of this unit.

The specimen tasks continue here with literary questions.

Literature and civilisation essays

The advice given for general essays applies equally to literature and civilisation essays. You should have studied the section of this unit entitled **Longer general essays** and also Task D, before you come to this section.

We do not have enough space here to give more than one specimen answer, so we have chosen a topic which relates the analysis of literary texts to an aspect of 'civilisation', here the role of women in society.

There is no room either for the treatment of context questions. These are not set by all Exam Boards in current syllabuses.

Additional advice is contained in the Examiner's commentary to Task E.

Wie sehen Sie das Verhältnis zwischen Frau und Gesellschaft?

Cambridge

TASK E

Here is another genuine candidate's answer. Approach it as you did Task D.

ANSWER

Ich glaube, daß das Verhältnis zwischen Frau und Gesellschaft nicht immer stark ist. Zuerst glaube ich, daß eine Frau oft ein Opfer ist, wegen unserer Gesellschaft. Ich bin der Meinung, daß man in einer Männerwelt wohnt[1], wo die Männer die führenden Positionen haben, zB. die Polizei und Journalisten in „Die verlorene Ehre der Katharina Blum", obwohl man erinnern muß, daß es manchmal Frauen sind, die andere Frauen ungerecht behandeln, nicht immer die Männer.

Zuerst denken Männer, daß eine Frau eine stereotypische Rolle in einer Gesellschaft (Männergesellschaft) hat, zB. macht Iphigenie in „Iphigenie in Tauris" ganz klar, daß Frauen immer das schwächere, zweite Geschlecht sein müssen. Ein Mann kann sich Ruhm und Lob durch kämpfen[2] und den Sieg im Krieg gewinnen. Er kann in allen Lebensbereichen erfolgreich sein. Aber für eine Frau bleibt nur das Gebiet der Ehe. Wenn sie die Ehe nicht hat, dann ist der Tod besser, deshalb ist die Ehe, und einem Mann zu gehorchen ihre einzige Rolle im Leben. Sie macht es ganz klar, wenn sie sagt „So hält mich Thoas hier, ein edler Mann, in ernsten, heil'gen Sklavenbanden fest. O wie beschämt gesteh ich, daß ich dir mit stillem Widerwillen diene, Göttin, Dir meiner Retterin!"

Goethe meint, daß die Milde die richtige Lebensart ist, nur durch diese Milde, diese Sanftheit, Treue und Wahrheit, die Iphigenie darstellt, kann die Welt im allgemeinen überhaupt gerettet werden. Und deshalb ist die Frau nicht immer ein Opfer. Einerseits sind die Männer in der Gesellschaft Opfern[3], weil sie immer beweisen wollen und sie nicht[4] die wichtigen Qualitäten haben, um die Welt zu verbessern.

Iphigenie, die Frauen darstellt, hat ein sehr positives[5] Einfluß auf der[6] Gesellschaft, und hier glaube ich, daß die Frau hat[7] ein sehr positives Verhältnis mit der Gesellschaft. Wir sehen die Grausamkeit und die Heldenlust der Männer und das steht gegenüber der Milde der Frauen. Thoas sagt „Solang die Rache meinen Geist besaß, empfand ich nicht die Öde meiner Wohnung". Die Frauen können die Situation von Opfern in der Gesellschaft umkehren, wegen ihres Einflußes[8]. Pylades sieht in Iphigenie die Hoffnung und die Liebe, die, laut Goethe, in allen Frauen vorhanden sind, die die einzige Hoffnung auf Freiheit und eine gute Zukunft bedeuten. Die Eigenschaft, die Iphigenie darstellt, erwecken[9] in Orest ein Bedürfnis nach Wahrheit. Orest sagt „zwischen uns sei Wahrheit". Der erste Tritt[10] zur Heilung geschieht durch Iphigenies Reinheit und Bedürfnis nach Wahrheit. Der nächste Tritt[10] geschieht durch ihre Liebe. Iphigenie sagt: „O laß den reinen Hauch der Liebe dir, die Glut des Busens leise Wehen kühlen." Auch wir[11] sehen das[5] Einfluß von Iphigenie auf Thoas, als er einen Waffenstillstand befielt[12]. Durch diesen Befehl macht Thoas den ersten Tritt[10] zum weiblichen Wesen. Das heißt „reden statt handeln". Hier ist das Verhältnis zwischen Frau und Gesellschaft gut, weil sie ein positives Einfluß[5] hat und sie kann die Welt verändern und retten. Andererseits sehen wir, daß Katharina ein Opfer der Gesellschaft ist. Hier ist das Verhältnis zwischen Frau und Gesellschaft nicht gut, weil die Gesellschaft Katharina zerstört – sie ist ein Opfer, aber ich glaube, daß sie ein Opfer ist, wegen der Männer, der Gesellschaft, der Einstellung der Gesellschaft und des Verfahrens.

Zuerst können wir sehen, daß Katharina ein Opfer ist, wegen der Behandlung von der Polizei, die keinen Respekt für Katharina hat, zB. die Demütigung von Katharina und die umstrittene Frage, die sich die Polizei mindestens überlegt hat oder gestellt hat: „Hat er dich denn gefickt?" Wir können auch sehen, daß sie ein Opfer der Männer ist. Sie glauben nur, daß Katharina ein Sexualobjekt ist und sie unterminieren sie. Sie denken nur über die Zudringlichkeit und nicht die Zärtlichkeit. Sie glauben, daß beide die gleichen[13] sind. Katharina war seit 14 Jahren alt[14] ein Opfer der Männer und hier glaube ich, daß die Gesellschaft schuldig ist. „Ja, nun müssen Sie nicht glauben, daß es etwas Neues für mich war, daß ein Mann mir an die Kledage wollte – wenn Sie von Ihrem vierzehnten Lebensjahr an, und schon früher, in Haushalten arbeiten, sind Sie was gewohnt." Katharina ist natürlich ein Opfer der Presse, und ich glaube, daß das nicht zu einem guten Verhältnis zwischen Frau und Gesellschaft führt. Die Journalisten haben die Wahrheit verdreht. Tötges muß über Katharina schreibt[15], um Sträubleder zu decken. Katharina wollte nicht mit Sträubleder schlafen und er war ungehalten, deshalb muß Katharina die Folge nehmen, wegen des Einflußes[8] von Sträubleder. Er manipuliert die Journalisten, weil er seinen Ruf nicht schädigen wollte. Er hat „die Zeitung" in der Hand. Ich glaube, daß hier Katharina ein Sündenbock und deshalb ein Opfer ist.

Besonders ist Katharina ein Opfer der Gesellschaft und ihrer Meinungen. Sie wollte nicht diese Rolle der Zudringlichkeit spielen, aber sie hat starke Morale[16] und Katharina glaubt an Zärtlichkeit, aber andere Leute denken, daß sie bös ist, zB. sie hat Briefe bekommen, die aus sexuellem Material bestanden. Jemand hat ihr alle möglichen Sex-Artikel geschickt und hat geschrieben: „Das sind die wahren Zärtlichkeiten." Katharina verliert alles, nicht nur ihre sexuelle Ehre, aber auch ihre Wohnung – alles, was sie gemacht hat, wegen der Gesellschaft. Hier ist die Gesellschaft nicht vorteilhaft für die Frau. Die Gesellschaft verursacht Katharina die Probleme, weil sie eine Frau ist. Ich glaube, daß Katharina nicht allein ist, und viele Frauen leiden wegen unserer Gesellschaft – sie werden Opfern[3].

Aber in „Iphigenie" können wir sehen, daß Frauen eine positive und selbstlose Einstellung zum Leben darstellen, während die Männer eine negative und egozentrische Einstellung zum Leben darstellen. Deshalb glaube ich, daß eine Frau ein sehr positives Einfluß[5] auf die Gesellschaft ausübt, aber oft wird sie ein Opfer wegen unsere[17] Männergesellschaft.

Examiner's commentary   The literary analysis shows sharp insight into the two texts upon which it is based and is expressed fluently in German. It is strictly related to the set question without any irrelevant comments or references. It presents the view of women as victims of society in the two works but shows that women do not merely have a passive, suffering role, like that of Katharina's, because they can turn this around and exert a positive influence on society like Iphigenie. Perhaps the candidate could have explored the extent to which Katharina is not simply a passive sufferer, the ways in which she asserts herself, for example during cross-examination by the police.

You will have noticed that errors are likely to creep into a timed essay where you are dealing with more complex ideas. This can happen more readily when you are not expressing your own ideas as such, as you would be in a general essay, but your opinion of an author's ideas. The important point to remember is that Exam Boards usually allocate at least half of the marks for content and often the bulk of the language marks for range of vocabulary, structures and idiom both in this type of essay and in Coursework assignments. The percentage of marks reserved for accuracy is therefore quite low. Indeed some Boards do not award language marks for this type of essay written in exam conditions. However, effective communication of abstract ideas is seriously hampered by inaccurate language, so your marks would be lowered generally by slapdash writing. This candidate's (relatively few) mistakes are indicated below, in case you missed any. Make sure you learn quotations properly and quote them accurately. If you have read the works to which the candidate refers in this answer, you may be able to correct some errors.

As for the essay on general topics, a plan is essential for good organisation. A clear structure is vital to help the examiner follow your argument, and may attract a certain percentage of the marks available, particularly for Coursework assignments.

Candidate errors corrected:

1 *in einer Männerwelt* **lebt.**

2 *Ein Mann kann Ruhm und Lob erkämpfen.*

3 *Opfer.*

4 *weil sie sich immer beweisen wollen aber nicht die wichtigen Qualitäten haben.*

5 **Der** *Einfluß,* so: *ein**en** sehr positiv**en** Einfluß,* and later: *auch sehen wir den Einfluß.*

6 *auf* **die** *Gesellschaft.*

7 Word order – verb at end of subordinate clause: *daß die Frau ein sehr positives Verhältnis mit der Gesellschaft* **hat.**

8 *Einflu**ss**es.*

9 *erweckt.*

10 *Schritt* **not** *Tritt.*

11 Inversion of subject and verb: *auch sehen wir den Einfluß.*

12 Spelling: *befieh**l**t.*

13 *daß beide gleich sind.*

14 *alt* should not be there: *seit 14 Jahren/seitdem sie 14 war.*

15 Infinitive: *schreiben.*

16 *sie hat starke Moral. Moral* (meaning 'morals') has no plural.

17 Genitive after *wegen*: *wegen unserer Männergesellschaft.*

EXAM PRACTICE

Before attempting any compositions in this section, you should have worked through the unit from the beginning, including the specimen tasks and answers, since the main advice you need to tackle questions has been given there. The Examiner's tips given here draw your attention briefly to common pitfalls.

For the length of each essay, follow your own Board's instructions.

Longer general compositions

Discursive essays (Exam Boards usually set proportionately more of these)

Medien
Die Gefahren und Lockungen von Horrorfilmen.

Cambridge

Haben Bücher im Fernsehzeitalter noch einen Platz?

NICCEA

Das Stadtleben
Der Mensch in der unbekannten Stadt.

Cambridge

Die Genetik
Ist es jetzt Zeit, mit der experimentellen Genetik Schluß zu machen?

Oxford and Cambridge

Examiner's tip Be careful not to be one-sided in these discursive essays. Be sure to present the opposing argument, even if you do not believe it has much validity.

Creative essays

„Wir waren also soweit: morgen war Generalprobe! Ich konnte nur hoffen, daß jeder seine Rolle gelernt hatte …" Erzählen Sie weiter.

Oxford and Cambridge

Schreiben Sie eine kurze Geschichte, die mit den folgenden Worten beginnt: „Ich saß jetzt zum allerersten Mal in einem deutschen Wagen auf einer deutschen Autobahn …"

NEAB

Schreiben Sie eine kurze Geschichte, die mit den folgenden Worten beginnt: „Ich hatte schon öfters vorher als Babysitter gearbeitet – aber niemals bei einer Familie mit neun Kindern! …"

NEAB

Examiner's tip Beware of tackling an imaginative composition if you have not had practice in doing so. Not liking other essay titles on the set paper is not a good enough reason for suddenly trying your hand at one of these. Story telling is an art in itself – just to mention a few hints: you need a clear and stimulating story line restricted to the relatively small number of words available and an interesting ending or outcome. What may seem an obvious and exciting plot or characterisation to you, may be confusing and tedious to somebody (the poor examiner) reading it. Another real danger here is to over-stretch yourself, letting your imagination run riot. Keep to what you can say in accurate German.

Essays based on a stimulus
See the Mixed Skills unit.

Newspaper or magazine articles
Schreiben Sie einen Artikel für eine deutsche Zeitschrift, in dem Sie erklären, warum Ausländer ihre Stadt bzw. ihre Gegend besuchen sollten.

Schreiben Sie einen Artikel für eine deutsche Zeitschrift, in dem Sie erklären, warum man entweder Vegetarier sein sollte, oder noch Fleisch essen sollte.

Examiner's tip Remember that it is for a newspaper or magazine, so the type of reader has to be borne in mind. In discursive essays you tend to write with your teacher or the examiner in mind, but here you are writing for a particular public. You are not so much weighing up two sides of a question as being polemical, trying to press home your own viewpoint on an issue of general concern.

Letters

„Liebe Gisela!

  Es tut mir leid, daß ich so lange nicht geschrieben habe. Inzwischen ist mir aber etwas Tolles passiert! Ich habe an einem Gewinnspiel teilgenommen und den ersten Preis gewonnen! 31000 habe ich gekriegt und natürlich schon ausgegeben!"

Du schreibst den Brief zu Ende. Erzähle deiner Brieffreundin, was du mit dem Geld gemacht hast!

SEB

Schreiben Sie einen Brief an eine deutsche Zeitung, in dem Sie gegen den Bau einer neuen Autobahn protestieren.

NEAB

Verfassen Sie einen Brief an den Bürgermeister von einer deutschen Stadt, in dem Sie sich über die mangelnden Freizeitmöglichkeiten beklagen.

Examiner's tip Make sure you distinguish between the informal and formal letter, both in opening and closing conventions and in the general tone you adopt. It helps to have had some practice at writing the various kinds of formal letter in English (in school lessons or in real life), to know for example how to approach writing to a newspaper or to a public official. In addition, you should have composed at least one letter of this type in German and had it corrected by your teacher.

Dialogues or monologues

„Ich verstehe das nicht, daß du am liebsten in Deutschland leben möchtest. In Großbritannien haben wir es doch viel besser!" Erfinden Sie ein Streitgespräch zwischen zwei jungen Menschen zu diesem Thema.

Oxford and Cambridge

Erfinden Sie ein Radio-Interview mit einem Menschen, der gerade eine Katastrophe überlebt hat.

NEAB

Mitten in der Nacht läutet bei Ihnen das Telefon. Sie nehmen den Hörer ab. Eine fremde Stimme sagt: „Ich muß das Geld haben. Ich komme gleich vorbei."

Erfinden Sie das Telefongespräch.

Examiner's tip What you are producing here is a script for a conversation, at which you need to have had some practice before the examination. Beware of attempting this, unless you have a good feeling for spoken German, particularly idiom. It must sound like normal speech when you read it back to yourself! Another problem is giving the dialogue some structure and development.

Literature and civilisation essays

Before attempting any compositions in this section, you should have worked through the earlier section of this unit entitled **Literature and civilisation essays**, including the specimen task and answers, since all the general advice you need to tackle questions has been given there. Extra advice given with each question is not specialised subject knowledge, but helps rather to avoid the potential pitfalls waiting for candidates who fail to grasp what exactly they have to do. It is vital to understand the meaning and impact of the German words in the essay question, which helps you to discover how to tackle it. Often what lets a candidate down is not lack of subject knowledge but the inability to put it to effective use in response to the question set.

For the length of each essay, follow your own Board's instructions.

We have not included questions set on one specific text, because set texts vary a great deal from one Exam Board to the other. Instead we have given questions on general literary or artistic themes and on aspects of Germany.

Die Nazizeit
Analysieren Sie anhand von Beispielen aus Ihrer Lektüre die Art und Weise, wie die Jugend durch den Nationalsozialismus beeinflußt wurde!

AEB

Examiner's tip The key words here are *anhand von Beispielen aus Ihrer Lektüre*. You are not required to summarise the influence of Nazi thinking on German youth of the time as a historian might. Each point you make must be based on the literary works you have studied. Moreover, avoid generalised statements. Give precise and detailed examples from the texts.

Die ehemalige DDR
Was waren, Ihrer Meinung nach, in den 80er Jahren die wichtigsten Ereignisse, die unmittelbar zu der Wende führten?

ULEAC

Examiner's tip The key words here are *die unmittelbar zu der Wende führten*. A summary of events in the DDR in the 1980s will gain no credit, unless you can show how they led **directly** to the *Wende*.

Das heutige Deutschland
Welche besonderen Probleme haben Kinder und Jugendliche aus Gastarbeiter- und Asylantenfamilien in der heutigen BRD?

ULEAC

Examiner's tip This is not an essay about the general problems of young people in Germany today. Nor should it merely be about *Ausländerfeindlichkeit*. Make sure that your discussion of problems such as *Arbeitslosigkeit* and *Obdachlosigkeit* relate strictly to the groups specified: *Gastarbeiter* and *Asylanten*. In which case you should mention *Flüchtlingslager* and *Ausländerwohnheime* and that *Asylrecht* is dependent on having *Arbeit und Wohnung*. Note also that it is the second generation, not the parents who are targeted by the question, so educational opportunities are a vital issue.

Das deutsche Schulsystem
Welche Aspekte des deutschen Schulsystems erregen heutzutage in Deutschland Besorgnis?

Oxford

Examiner's tip You should not tackle specific questions like this one, unless you have very detailed and up-to-date subject knowledge. The key word is *Besorgnis*. Get straight to the point and deal only with aspects causing concern at the present time.

Welche Aspekte des deutschen Schulsystems finden Sie besonders gut? Bewerten Sie ihren Erfolg und analysieren Sie die Gründe dafür.

Oxford

Examiner's tip As for the previous essay, but now you must select the aspects of the system which have been successful, and also evaluate and explain their success.

Eine Gegend oder eine Stadt
Es scheint oft, daß sich alle Städte und alle Gegenden immer mehr ähneln. Stimmt dies für die von Ihnen studierte Stadt oder Gegend oder besitzt sie noch ihren eigenen Charakter?

Oxford

Examiner's tip The danger of such essays is that you can sink into generalisation. You would be advised not to tackle this question unless you can think of unique characteristics of your chosen town or region. These should be the focus of your answer. The way it resembles other places is best summarised in your introduction, before you go on to show how it is different.

Bewerten Sie die Entwicklungen in den letzten 10–15 Jahren in Ihrer gewählten Region! Haben Sie Veränderungen zum Guten bzw. Schlechten verursacht?

AEB

Examiner's tip A good knowledge of the recent history of your chosen town or region is needed to pick out exactly what has changed. Then you need to weigh the good against the bad (not being too negative or too uncritical) in order to make an overall conclusion. Answers like this are often wrongly left in the air. A good response will come down on one side at the end (but **not** at the beginning – this makes for uninteresting reading!).

Die Medien
Bewerten Sie die Entwicklungen im deutschen Fernsehen in den 90er Jahren!

AEB

Examiner's tip Make sure you concentrate on the developments, not merely the cable and satellite provision with the plethora of programmes, but also on new types of programme. The word *bewerten* is crucial: analyse the quantity/quality equation. You might consider how German television is adapting to the changes in comparison with British television.

Wählen Sie eine große deutsche Nationalzeitung. Was sind die Stärken und Schwächen dieser Zeitung?

Oxford

Examiner's tip Home in on the strengths and weaknesses, but try to be objective at the same time as giving your personal views: the essay should not be biased towards your own political, social or other ideas.

Der deutsche Film

Inwiefern ist der Fassbinder Film, den Sie zum eingehenden Studium gewählt haben für seine Filmkunst typisch? Begründen Sie Ihre Antwort.

ULEAC

Analysieren Sie den Einfluß der Gesellschaft auf die Hauptfiguren in Ihren gewählten Filmen!

AEB

Examiner's tip You could apply these two questions to any film producer you have studied. In the first, you are supposed to pick out the main themes and characteristics of the producer and illustrate these with reference to your chosen film. At least, you need to have studied criticism of other films (preferably to have seen at least one or two). Good answers would also point out unique aspects of the chosen film. The second question is tricky, unless you have detailed knowledge of society at the time of the film.

Die Kunst

Was ist originell im Werk des von Ihnen studierten Künstlers und was verdankt er der Tradition?

Oxford

Inwiefern wird die Leistung des von Ihnen studierten Künstlers durch die Zeit, in der er lebt, bedingt oder beeinflußt?

Oxford

Examiner's tip Both essays require you to analyse the originality of your chosen artist, the first in relation to what (s)he owes to tradition and the second by reference to what (s)he acquired and adapted from contemporary events. *Bedingt* implies more limitation upon the artist's originality than *beeinflußt*, so you need to consider to what extent the artist was able to rise above the times.

Familienverhältnisse
Ohne Familie muß der Einzelmensch notwendigerweise zugrunde gehen.

Cambridge

(Kafka: *Das Urteil*; Fontane: *Effi Briest*; Hauptmann: *Einsame Menschen*; Horváth: *Geschichten aus dem Wiener Wald*.)

Gerechtigkeit und das Gesetz
Das Gesetz dient der Gesellschaft und den Machthabern, nicht dem Einzelnen.

Cambridge

(Brecht: *Der kaukasische Kreidekreis*; Dürrenmatt: *Der Richter und sein Henker*; Hochwälder: *Das heilige Experiment* OR *Der öffentliche Ankläger*; Kleist: *Das Erdbeben in Chili* OR *Michael Kohlhaas*.)

Examiner's tip The two thematic questions above might be applicable to some of the books set by your Board or which you have read out of interest. The works to which they applied in the actual examination paper are given in brackets after each question. For your book(s) consider also the implications of the **reverse** of what is suggested by the two titles. In other words: is the family actually able to support the individual? What are the dangers of the course of justice being perverted by individual citizens? You don't have to assume that the statement in the title is correct!

Some Exam Boards set mixed skill papers combining Reading, Listening and Writing tasks. A written task could be based either on a Reading or a Listening stimulus or on both. The same ability to understand the written and spoken word is being tested as in discreet (individual) skill papers. To perform well on these mixed papers, you simply need to be able to approach individual Reading and Listening questions as shown in the appropriate unit in this book. You then need to bear in mind the points made in the Writing unit about written assignments. The fact that the skills are mixed in one module or paper will help you to the extent that there will be common topics and themes across the skills, so there will be less jumping from one subject to another.

In order to help you prepare for a mixed skill approach, we have printed composition topics below based on a stimulus which is to be found in this book or on the accompanying CD/cassette. The reference in brackets [ ] is to the appropriate unit of the book with its task, and sometimes to the Speaking section of the CD/cassette, which you can use as a listening stimulus for this purpose. First carry out the tasks in those units, then read or listen to the stimulus again, as appropriate, before answering these questions. The compositions are of various types. You may use words and expressions from the stimulus material, but you should not copy whole phrases or sentences.

Before attempting any compositions in this unit, you should also have worked through the Writing unit from the beginning, including the specimen Writing tasks and answers.

For the length of each essay, follow your own Board's instructions.

Süchte [Listening Tasks F and M]
„Jeder ist von irgendeinem Genuß- oder Rauschmittel abhängig. Es ist ganz normal, süchtig zu sein."
„Zu viele Jugendliche sind alkohol- oder drogenabhängig. Die Regierung sollte strengere Maßnahmen gegen diese Mißbräuche treffen."
Nehmen Sie Stellung zu diesen unterschiedlichen Gesichtspunkten.

Kriminalität [Listening Tasks H and Q]
„Die meisten Kriminellen sind unverbesserlich. Man braucht längere Freiheitsstrafen, um die Gesellschaft gegen diese Verbrecher zu schützen."
„Es hat keinen Sinn, einen Kriminellen auf viele Jahre ins Gefängnis einzusperren. Man sollte versuchen, ihn auszubilden und zu bessern."
Nehmen Sie Stellung zu diesen unterschiedlichen Gesichtspunkten.

Examiner's tip
For your answer to the two essays above you need to see the question from both sides, for instance on crime the need for society to punish the criminal as a deterrent, as well as its duty to reform him or her. If you have strong personal views on crime or on drugs, leave these to your conclusion, when you weigh up the pros and cons.

Die Umwelt [Listening Task L, Reading Tasks I/J and Speaking CD/cassette Sections 3/4]
„Es hat keinen Zweck, Gesetze einzuführen, um die Umwelt zu schützen. Unsere Welt geht sowieso kaputt. Wir können nichts dagegen machen."
„Wenn sich jeder sofort für die Umwelt einsetzen würde, könnte man die Umwelt noch vor allen Lastern retten."
Nehmen Sie Stellung zu diesen unterschiedlichen Gesichtspunkten.

Schreiben Sie einen Brief an den Umweltminister Deutschlands, in dem Sie strengere Umweltgesetze fordern.

> **Examiner's tip** For the first title, see the tip for the essays on crime/drugs. For the second refer back to the tips on letter-writing in the Writing unit. Listening to the Speaking CD/cassette will give you some ideas and vocabulary.

Das Schulsystem: [Listening Task I and Reading Task B]
„Die Schule bietet keine gute Ausbildung für das Leben."

Warum gibt es, Ihrer Meinung nach, in unserer modernen Gesellschaft so viele Analphabeten?

> **Examiner's tip** In both the above essays, beware of being over-critical of the educational system. Consider also the other (social) reasons for poor school performance/illiteracy.

Schreiben Sie einen Artikel für die Schülerzeitung Ihrer deutschen Partnerschule, in dem Sie das Schulsystem in Ihrem Land mit dem deutschen Schulsystem vergleichen.

> **Examiner's tip** You might like to listen again to Listening Task K about a German school magazine. Try not to be merely descriptive. The German readers will know about their system, so concentrate on how the English one differs, giving your opinions about which you think is better and why.

Arbeit und Ausbildung [Listening Task T, Reading Tasks D and P, and Speaking CD/cassette Section 5]
Was könnte man sonst noch tun, um die Zahl der Arbeitslosen zu reduzieren?

> **Examiner's tip** Listening to the Speaking CD/cassette will give you some ideas and vocabulary. You will have to mention what measures are already in place and how effective they are, before saying what else you think should be done and why.

Ausländerfeindlichkeit [Listening Task N]
Schreiben Sie einen Artikel für eine deutsche Zeitschrift, in dem Sie sich zum Thema von Ausländerfeindlichkeit in Deutschland äußern!

> **Examiner's tip** Before you are too scathing about German treatment of foreigners, compare the German problem with racial issues in the UK. Could we learn from each other?

Verkehrsmittel [Listening Task S, Reading Task J and Speaking CD/cassette Sections 3/4]
Erfinden Sie ein Gespräch zwischen einem Jugendlichen, der immer mit dem Rad oder mit den öffentlichen Verkehrsmitteln fährt, und seinem Vater, der auf seinen Wagen nicht verzichten will.

> **Examiner's tip** A good opportunity to express two distinct viewpoints. This is always easier when you have to express your ideas through two opposing characters. Listening to the Speaking CD/cassette will help you with the conversational structures needed to persuade others to adopt your point of view, and of course to come to a compromise.

Kriegsdienst oder Zivildienst? [Listening Task P]

Erfinden Sie ein Gespräch, das Sie mit einem jungen Deutschen führen, der entscheiden soll, ob er Kriegs- oder Zivildienst leisten wird.

Examiner's tip It might be easier to take one viewpoint, for military service, and let the friend put the case for community service (or vice-versa), before deciding which to choose. The decision should be based upon the discussion. You might give your views on the value of this idea of service for the UK.

Hausfrau oder Karrierefrau? [Listening Task R and Reading Tasks F and N]

Erfinden Sie ein Gespräch zwischen einem Deutschen, der meint, daß Frauen eher zu Hause bleiben sollte, um sich mit den Kindern und der Hausarbeit zu beschäftigen, und seiner Freundin, die Karrierefrau werden will.

Examiner's tip It is fun to write an argument between two extremists, but perhaps there should be room for compromise!

Technologie [Reading Task G]

Schreiben Sie einen Brief an einen Freund, der Angst vor Computern, Faxgeräten usw. hat, und versuchen Sie ihn zu überzeugen, daß ihm die neue Technologie sehr nützlich sein könnte.

Examiner's tip Only to be tackled if you are a modern technology buff. Beware of writing about topics of which you have insecure knowledge and no strong interest.

Das Alter: [Reading Task E]

Schreiben Sie einen Brief an eine ältere Verwandte, die sich nicht entscheiden kann, ob sie in ein Altersheim gehen oder noch in ihren eigenen vier Wänden leben sollte.

Examiner's tip Try not to be too negative about old people's homes. Avoid condescension, be sympathetic, and remember that the old lady is a relative, so you should express your feelings as well as your ideas and show some involvement/commitment.

Als „Single" leben oder heiraten? [Listening Task O]

„Der Ehestand bringt mehr Nachteile als Vorteile."
Sind Sie auch dieser Meinung?

Examiner's tip Again, you have to see both points of view, but you don't have to agree with the proposition.

Das Abenteuer [Reading Task C]

Schreiben Sie eine kurze Geschichte, die mit den folgenden Worten beginnt: „Es war die erste Woche meiner Reise durch Europa, und mein Geld war schon alle."

Examiner's tip Refer to the tip on Creative essays in the Writing unit.

Answers

LISTENING ANSWERS

Task		Answer	Mark
A	**1**	australisch	1
	2	Radsport	1
	3	(sie hatte) kein gültiges Visum	1
	4	(mit dem) Flugzeug/(sie ist) geflogen	1
	5	wertvolle Medaillen [Note pronunciation!]	2
	6	weil ihre Identität festgestellt wurde/war	1

> **Examiner's tip**
>
> **1/2** You need to listen very attentively at the start: the first two answers come **before** the mention of Kathy Watts by name. Did you have the right sound but the wrong meaning (*Rat*) in **2**?
>
> **4** You have to work the answer from *auf dem Flughafen*.
>
> **6** After hearing the answer to **6**, you have to ignore a long redundant sentence. Not all the material you hear will be necessary for your answers. Learn how to keep to the point.

Task		Answer	Mark
B	**1**	has reduced interest rates (1) by $\frac{1}{2}$% (1).	2
	2	will **not** be shut down.	1
	3	has decided that one does **not** have to declare (to the authorities) (1) if one has Aids (1).	2
	4	has critically injured a 24-year-old student.	1

> **Examiner's tip**
>
> **1** The key word is *Leitzinssenkungen*. If you heard *geschlossen* instead of *beschlossen*, you may have thought that the money markets were closed. Learn prefixes to *schließen*. See **3**.
>
> **2** Did you fail to hear the negative *nicht*? Like **3** this answer seems more plausible in a positive form. Avoid guessing!
>
> **3** *Meldepflicht* = obligation to notify the authorities. The key word is *ausgeschlossen* = ruled out.
>
> **4** If you miss *ein ... Jahre alter*, you will think 24 students were killed.

Task		Answer	Mark
C	**1**	D	1
	2	C	1
	3	B	1
	4	A	1

> **Examiner's tip**
>
> You need to listen out for the types of weather given in written form, then to the region which follows. Answer B is mentioned with *Norden und Westen* meaning the North and the West, so the detail you hear at this point is for the West (**not** the Northwest which came first). *böige* = gusty/squally.

Letts
Q&A

Task		Answer	Mark
D	1	Rhine Valley (1); Lake Constance (1).	2
	2	Around zero/freezing.	1
	3	Queen of Denmark (1); her husband/Prince Henrik (1).	2
	4	New German states (those formerly in DDR).	1
	5	Nurses (1) for better working conditions (1).	2
	6	More than 5.3 million (recorded) (1); less than half (solved) (1).	2
	7	Violence (1); drug-related crimes (1).	2

Examiner's tip

1 *die Niederungen* = flats/marshland.

2 *der Gefrierpunkt* = freezing point.

5 *Bedingungen* = conditions; *Tarifverhandlungen* = pay talks; *scheitern* = to collapse.

6 In German the decimal point is expressed as a comma (*Komma*); *aufklären* = to solve (crime).

Task		Answer	Mark
E	1	mit Reisen/unterwegs	1
	2	[weil] in meinem Bekanntenkreis kein Spender ist	1
	3	[wenn] ich morgen auf der Straße liege/ [wenn] ich einen Unfall habe	1
	4	[daß es] einen per Brief zum Spenden einlädt	1

Examiner's tip

2/3 Notice that you have to manipulate the German, not transcribe it. The sentences you hear have to be turned around. The subordinate clause which you have to give in the answers, starting *weil/wenn*, comes **before** the main clause provided for you at the start of each answer, *Ich verbringe ... /Ich fühle ...*

4 You must change the passive construction *daß sie eingeladen werden* into an active one with the subject *es*.

Task		Answer	Mark
F	1	False	1
	2	True	1
	3	True	1
	4	False	1

Examiner's tip

1 The figure of $2\frac{1}{2}$ million refers to the number of alcohol addicts. *die Sucht* = addiction.

2 There are 17 million smokers but only 6 million need treatment.

3 Listen for cue: **Noch nicht** *mit Zahlen belegen kann die Organisation zwei weitere Abhängigkeiten; belegen* = verify.

4 *überwiegend* = predominantly/mainly.

There is a composition linked to this Listening stimulus (and that of Task M) in the Mixed Skills unit.

Listening answers

Task		Answer	Mark
G	1	handeln/Handel treiben	1
	2	fliegen	1
	3	Investoren (1) Touristen (1) **oder** Geschäftsleute/Kaufleute (1)	2
	4	wirtschaftliche (1) Reformen (1)	2
	5	den Süden (1) Chinas (1)	2

Task		Answer	Mark
H	1	[some] 6000	1
	2	[because of] grievous bodily harm/assault	1
	3	[only] 152	1
	4	[cases of] officers drinking on duty	1
	5	[About] 400,000	1
	6	[Association of] insurance salesmen/brokers	1
	7	[increased] premiums/insurance costs	1
	8	[unless] one pays an additional premium	1

Task		Answer	Mark
I	1	Sie ist von der Realschule aufs Gymnasium gegangen.	1
	2	(1 mark each for any **two** of:) schlecht, streng, nicht nett, ziemlich unorganisiert.	2
	3	Die Lehrer waren nett/toll (1) lustig (1).	2
	4	Der Standard war höher (1); es war ein großer Sprung von der 10. zur 11. Klasse (1); die Lehrer waren unfreundlich (1).	3

Task		Answer	Mark
J		Answers are given in the order in which they are heard. One mark for each point up to a maximum of 7.	
	1	Shaped like a bee-hive.	**1**
	2	Has been hanging for a few centuries in tower of St. Catherine's/in church ruins.	**1**
	3	Can't be pulled/rung or moved.	**1**
	4	Can only be struck.	**1**
	5	It is struck once a year at the Lullus festival.	**1**
	6	On one occasion when it was rung the tower collapsed.	**1**
	7	Oldest **dated** bell in Germany.	**1**
	8	Dated 1038.	**1**

> **Examiner's tip** There is a certain amount of background noise which makes the listening situation authentic. You need to learn to cope with this.
>
> **1** *Bienenkorb* = bee-hive.
>
> **3** *läuten* = to ring (a bell); *beweglich* = movable (but listen for negative *nicht mehr* before this word).
>
> **6** *zusammenbrechen* = to collapse.
>
> **7** There is a bell which is possibly older, from the 10th century (*Jahrhundert*), but that one is not dated.
>
> **8** Note *tausend* to express years which begin with 'ten' in English, e.g. 1066.

Task		Answer	Mark
K		Answers are given in the order in which they are heard. You need all five for full marks.	
	1	über Themen, die die Schule betreffen	**1**
	2	über weltpolitische Sachen	**1**
	3	über Kultur	**1**
	4	über kommunale Sachen (= local matters)	**1**
	5	über Sachen, die man nicht unbedingt in der Tagespresse erfährt	**1**

> **Examiner's tip** There is a little lead-in before you reach the material you want. The vocabulary here is not unduly hard, but you will need to take notes as you hear each point. There is slight 'padding' between some points to give you time to do so. There is no mark for mentioning *um Leute zu aktivieren/informieren* since most articles should fall into this heading anyway.
>
> **4** Did you hear/write *kriminale* here? The adjective is in fact *kriminell*. *Der Kriminale* (**noun** declined as adjective) = CID officer.
>
> **5** This is the most taxing, particularly since you must render the qualified negative *nicht unbedingt* = not necessarily.

Task		Answer	Mark
L	**1**	[Menschen] bei den Behörden	1
	2	[stationär] (= as in-patient) behandelt werden	2
	3	[wegen des] Verdachts der Umweltgefährdung	2

Examiner's tip
It is possible to do this task purely phonetically by transcribing the sounds you hear. However, you are much more likely to get it right, if you **understand** the words you are writing. To do this you need to comprehend the overall situation in the gapped text by reading it thoroughly **before** you hear the tape. Your grammar and spelling needs to be accurate!

3 This means '(on) suspicion of endangering the environment'.

There is a composition linked to this Listening stimulus (and to Reading Tasks I/J and the oral examination on the CD/cassette Sections 3 and 4) in the Mixed Skills unit.

Task		Answer	Mark
M	**1**	immer weitere Kreise	2
	2	Bundesgesundheitsministerium	1
	3	zur Verfügung stellen	2

Examiner's tip
Procedure as for the previous Task (L).

1 *weite Kreise ziehen* = to have wide repercussions.

3 This means 'put at the disposal (of the *Länder*)'.

There is a composition linked to this Listening stimulus (and that of Task F) in the Mixed Skills unit.

Task		Answer	Mark
N	**1**	She feels partly German (1) partly Turkish (1).	2
	2	It is hard to get a job (1) even with a good school report (1).	2
	3	They said she was just like them (i.e. German) (1) but she considers herself a Turk (1).	2
	4	An 18- or 19-year-old/a young neo-Nazi (1) (who) was totally against foreigners (1) used a racist/defamatory word (*Kanacke*) to refer to Turks (1); said he could smell a Turk one kilometre away against the wind (1); when she told him she was a Turk (1) he turned around and walked away (1).	6

Examiner's tip
We are moving into the longer passages. You need to make mental notes, because you hear this without a break. In this item the vocabulary is not too demanding, but you need to follow the flow of expression of the girl's feelings for the first three questions and then give an accurate narrative account for the last question.

2 The material you need comes at the end of Dilara's first speech.

4 Each point has to be full and correct for a mark. This will test your ability to render detail.

There is a composition linked to this Listening stimulus in the Mixed Skills unit.

Task		Answer	Mark
O	1	**Any two of**: You don't have to tell anyone where you are going and when you are coming back (1); nobody to be bothered by socks or newspapers you leave lying about (1); nobody to be annoyed that you don't often (help to) clean the flat/house (1).	2
	2	Have they taken a firm decision to live alone?/do they live alone because they are convinced it's the best way to live? (1); or are they single through lack of opportunity? (1).	2
	3	Can go to see 'David Copperfield' (1) and pay DM 150 for the ticket (1).	2
	4	Being single would have been seen as strange (*komisch*) (1); it wasn't right (*nicht stimmen*) (1); people thought you couldn't find a partner (*abkriegen* = make a conquest) (1); it used to be a stigma (*Makel*) but now it's considered normal (1).	4

Examiner's tip

1 There is no lead-in; you should find the answer immediately.

2 If you get lost, listen for the intonation of the voice for the question you need to render.

4 This demands detail like the last question of Task N. If you knew all the vocabulary here and how to render it in English, you should do well!

There is a composition linked to this Listening stimulus in the Mixed Skills unit.

Task		Answer	Mark
P	1	Es paßte nicht zu ihm (den Kriegsdienst zu leisten (1); es entspricht seiner Person/Persönlichkeit, Zivildienst zu machen (1); er will nicht lernen, andere Menschen zu töten/auf andere Menschen zu schießen (1).	3
	2	Er müßte sich eine Zivildienststelle besorgen.	1
	3	Er denkt, daß es eine sinnvolle Tätigkeit ist (1) weil er Medizin studiert (1).	2
	4	seit einem halben Jahr/seit sechs Monaten.	1
	5	Blut abnehmen (1); Spritze setzen (1).	2
	6	einen stinknormalen/langweiligen (1) langen (1) Tag.	2
	7	Er hat 10 Tage hintereinander Dienst (1) und (erst) dann 4 Tage frei (1).	2

Examiner's tip

You are now expected to write some longer answers in German. With a long passage, it may seem quicker for you to make notes in English to get all the details down. Resist this temptation! You will have trouble retranslating everything for the answers.

1 Did you hear *sprechen*? Achim uses **ent**sprechen – note the prefix – meaning 'to be in keeping with'. Did you lose the third mark by missing *nicht* again? If you make your answers logical in relation to the question, you won't make such mistakes anyway!

2 It is not enough to say that he is told he has to do *Zivildienst* (community service). This is obvious to Achim. *Einberufung* = call-up.

5 Cue: listen for the words *bis auf* = except.

6 The idea of *lang* comes from *der zieht sich* = it drags on.

There is a composition linked to this Listening stimulus in the Mixed Skills unit.

Listening answers

Task		Answer	Mark
Q	1	F	1
	2	R	1
	3	F (*nach wie vor angespannt*)	1
	4	F (real answer is 29)	1
	5	R (*die strikte Nachrichtensperre wird aufrechterhalten* = news embargo maintained)	1
	6	R	1
	7	F (only two – we hear later that one of the three was left behind)	1
	8	R (*gefesselt*)	1
	9	F (Did you miss the negative *un-* in *unbestätigt*?)	1
	10	F (*mit unbekanntem Ziel* – unknown destination)	1
	11	R (*sollen die Forderungen der Täter erfüllt worden sein*)	1
	12	R	1

> **Examiner's tip**
>
> **3/4** The answer you need for **4** comes before the information needed for **3** is finished.
>
> **7/8/9** These are intertwined. You will have to unravel them together. Some things are confirmed, but unfortunately **not** what is mentioned in **9**. Listen for the context, not just a key word.
>
> **10** We will have to wait for later reports to see if the police have discovered the gangsters' whereabouts.

R	1	Unsinn (1); sie erklärt ihnen, daß es Mädchen genausogut können wie Jungs (1).	2
	2	Sie sind es nicht gewohnt, daß Frauen an Autos arbeiten.	1
	3	Sie hat an Fahrrädern/an Mofas (he)rumgebastelt.	1
	4	bei einem Arzt.	1
	5	4 Wochen (vierwöchig).	1
	6	Eine Kupplung (=clutch) (1) ist ihr auf die Finger gefallen (1).	2
	7	einen schweren Motor (1) oder ein Getriebe (=gear-box) zu heben (1) **or:** weil die Arbeit schwer ist (1) und eine Frau muß kräftig sein (1).	2
	8	Ein Mädchen es genausogut schaffen kann wie ein Junge (1); für sie ist das kein Problem/sie kommt gut damit klar (1).	2
	9	wie die anderen/ganz normal.	1
	10	die Eltern (1) Vorurteile haben (1).	2
	11	[wollte] sich im Betrieb von ihrem Vater ausbilden lassen (1) [aber ihr Vater] sagte, „Nein, bei uns nehmen wir keine Mädchen." (or reported speech)/sagte, daß sie etwas anderes machen sollte (1).	2
	12	[daß] Hilde die nächste Inspektion (=service) bei ihren Autos machen könnte.	1

Task	Answer	Mark

Examiner's tip

1 There is a long lead-in before Hilde's speech, so did you miss her first word *Unsinn*?

3 Her interest in cars came after her childhood, through her boyfriend (*Freund*).

4 Did you hear *Lehrer* instead of *Lehre* = apprenticeship?

8 If you mentioned *daß es sogar ein Junge nicht allein schaffen kann* you are stating fact instead of **opinion**.

12 You need to report their speech – note use of subjunctive.

There is a composition linked to this Listening stimulus (and to Reading Tasks F and N) in the Mixed Skills unit.

S   Answers are given in the order in which they are heard:

Covers Graubünden district/South East Switzerland (1).
Mountainous terrain (1); 400 kilometre network (1).
Goes through various types of scenery (1).
Glacier and Bernina express on same network (1).
Carries people from outside Switzerland (1).
Offers genuine travel experience (1).
Used by business people (1).
Some use it purely as a means of getting to places (1); but mainly a tourist railway (1).
Acts as an express train for tourists (1).
Carries local (*einheimisch*) people (1).
Transports goods (*Güter*) (1).
All-purpose (*universell*) means of transport (1).   **14**

Examiner's tip

Die Rhätische Bahn = Rhaetian railway.

Erschließungsbahn = railway which develops the infrastructure of the canton.

This item is good practice for listening to a Swiss accent. You need **all** the points mentioned. If you were successful without having to pause the tape several times or replaying the item a few times, you are a genius!

There is a composition linked to this Listening stimulus (and to Reading Task J) in the Mixed Skills unit.

T   **1**   There were many unemployed people (1); some wanted to help/support the unemployed (1) or to set up a group/centre where they could talk about their problems (1).   **3**

2   It had to be set up on a professional basis.   **1**

3   loneliness (1) despair (1) guilt (1).   **3**

4   They find it hard to talk about themselves/they are less open than women.   **1**

5   They find unemployment a particular stigma.   **1**

Task		Answer	Mark
	6	They can speak as long as they like for a one unit telephone charge (within Hamburg).	**1**
	7	Through (ZDF) television broadcasts.	**1**
	8	The face-to-face advice lasts longer (one and a half hours) so can include discussion of (social security) benefits and advice (about debts/pensions).	**1**
	9	No files/records are kept.	**1**

Examiner's tip

1 *Anlaufstelle* = drop-in/advice centre.

2 Cue: *im Laufe der Zeit. freiwillig* = voluntary.

3 Cue: *im psychischen Bereich. vereinsamen* = to become lonely.

4 There is a long lead-in before the cue: *Männer, so würde ich sagen.*

5 For *Makel* see Task O.

8 *Rentenberatung* = pensions advice.

9 *Strichliste* = checklist.

There is a composition linked to this Listening stimulus (and to Reading Tasks D/P and the oral examination on the CD/cassette Section 5) in the Mixed Skills unit.

READING ANSWERS

Task		Answer	Mark
A	**2**	Die Taxifirma	**1**
	3	Wolfgang Zimmerer	**1**
	4	Paul Paschke	**1**
	5	Paul Paschke	**1**
	6	Paul Paschke	**1**
	7	Paul Paschke	**1**
	8	Jennifer Zimmerer	**1**

Examiner's tip

die Wehen setzten ein	= she went into labour
die Katastrophenschutzübung	= disaster control exercise
wohlbehalten	= safe and sound

Check whether the first question is done for you as an example, as here, in order to avoid wasting time working it out. It is important to notice the taxi driver's name, Paul Paschke, in the opening paragraph. The captions under the pictures help you with Questions **5** and **7**. The answers to Questions **5** and **6** come the other way round in the text, in the last sentence of the third paragraph. All the names in the grid are used, although Barbara's merely in the example and only Paul Paschke is involved more than once. Don't be afraid to keep crossing the same box!

Letts
Q&A

Task			Answer	Mark
B	**1**		When another customer comes she puts anything in her trolley (1); she pretends to have left her glasses behind (1); she bandages up her hand (1); others fill in forms for her (1).	**4**
	2	(a)	Classes too big (1); parents have no time to help (1); parents are illiterate (1).	**3**
		(b)	She hardly went to school (1); left at 14 (1).	**2**
	3		Ordered items which are on every menu (1); made up stories when reading books with her children (1); made sure that husband helped with children's homework.	**3**
	4	(a)	Out of fear of not getting a job.	**1**
		(b)	Gain in self-confidence (1); ability to do things by themselves/being independent (1).	**2**
		(c)	To write her own address (1); to write a postcard herself to her eldest daughter (1).	**2**

Examiner's tip Where you have to give answers in English (as in this task and in Tasks C and D) Exam Boards tend to remind you not to translate the text but to give all relevant details.

This is a task where you have to read the text particularly carefully before looking at the questions, since the points you need do not come in a neat sequence. You need to know where to find them in the text.

1 The first point of the answer comes in the first paragraph, the other points in the fourth.

2(a) See paragraph 6.

3 See paragraphs 7 and 8.

4(a)/(b) These points are arguably interchangeable. There is also the stimulus of helping children with homework.

There is a composition linked to this Reading stimulus in the Mixed Skills unit.

Task		Answer	Mark
C	**1**	She hitchhiked from the motorway intersection in the Rhein-Main area (1) taking 36 hours in a dozen stages (1) in bouncy Citroën 2CVs and in rickety vans (1).	**3**
	2	Worn out/overtired (1); hungry (1).	**2**
	3	No money for accommodation (1); cash and documents stolen (1); had to camp in the open in cold and rain (1).	**3**
	4	In a scrap with a lorry-driver who was forcing his company on her (1) she smashed her watch (1).	**2**
	5	Not yet 18 (1); short of money (1); often robbed (1).	**3**
	6	Any **two** of: Getting to know other countries/people (1); sharing experiences (1); cheap (1).	**2**

Reading answers

Task	Answer	Mark

Examiner's tip

1 The idea of hitchhiking is made clear by the word *Tramper*. *schaukeln* = (of car) bump up and down; *klapprig* = shaky.

3 *das Festgewühl* = crowd/throng.

4 If you put 'No food and drink', you ignored the question wording: 'What happened?' *das Handgemenge* = scuffle; *aufdringlich* = pushy/insistent.

5 *minderjährig* = who is still a minor, (opposite = *volljährig*); *knapp bei Kasse* = barely enough cash to get by.

There is a composition linked to this Reading stimulus (and to the oral examination on the CD/cassette Section 5) in the Mixed Skills unit.

D	1	Slept badly (1); woken twice by police (1); had to show his documents (1); and answer questions (1).	**4**
	2	The gas for his stove ran out.	**1**
	3	Of being sent back to his own country/to Poland.	**1**
	4	They go down by the docks and line up (on kerb or roadside) (to offer themselves for employment) (1); skilled labourers in trucks drive slowly past them to eye them up (1); give a nod/a wave (1); and the workers (bend down and) negotiate their pay through the open (truck) window (1).	**4**
	5 (a)	Some have worked for months without pay.	**1**
	(b)	He had his employer's address so that he could threaten to beat him up (if he was not paid).	**1**
	6	They were converting attics (1); the foreman unscrewed the door handles every night (1) to lock them in (1); they slept on mattresses amid rubble (1); during the day only one was allowed off the building site to shop (1).	**5**
	7	Last year on a motorway service area near Schwerin (1) some youths forced him to speak to them (1); he had to say that Hitler was good (1).	**3**

Examiner's tip

jemanden um etwas bringen	= to do somebody out of something
sich quälen	= to struggle
ausgehen	= to run out
verzehren	= to consume
lauern	= to lie in wait/lurk
ein Arbeitsstrich	= people lined up offering themselves for work
der Pritsch(en)wagen	= platform truck
der Betrüger	= swindler
schuften	= to slave away
der Auftraggeber	= employer
der Griff (-e)	= handle
der Bauschutt	= building rubble
nötigen	= to compel
stottern	= to stutter

It is necessary to select the required information from the text, discarding irrelevant points. Be careful not to translate whole sections.

Task	Answer	Mark

1 Notice which details were needed from the first paragraph.

2 *ausgehen* does not mean that the gas has gone out!

3 *nach Hause* does not mean home in the sense of his house.

4/6 Be careful to make as many points as there are marks available. Note that the language of the text highlights the degrading situation in which the workers are placed. In **4** the writer hints at a parallel with prostitution.

There is a composition linked to this Reading stimulus (and to Reading Task P, Listening Task T and the oral examination on the CD/cassette Section 5) in the Mixed Skills unit.

E	2	F		1
	3	I		1
	4	N		1
	5	H		1
	6	K	(*Pflegeheim* = nursing home)	1
	7	M		1
	8	D		1
	9	J		1
	10	L		1
	11	E		1
	12	A		1
	13	G		1

Examiner's tip

wack(e)lig	= wobbly/shaky
die Sozialstation	= social security office
eine wunde Stelle verarzten	= patch up/bandage a sore
mehr Einsätze (here)	= a greater deployment of staff
in Schuß halten	= keep in good shape
einen Acker bewirtschaften	= to work the land
auswandern	= to emigrate
die Vertrautheit	= intimacy/close relationship
es drängt die Zeit	= time is pressing
immerhin	= at any rate/at least/after all
examiniert	= qualified
Spritzen verabreichen	= administer injections
betten	= to make a bed for somebody
lagern	= to bed down/lay (somebody) down in bed

Here it is best to read the *Anfänge* and *Endungen* before you study the text. Note from the rubric that some endings are spare. Count them! In fact only one is. Even without reading the text you can see that there are in the case of each beginning of a sentence only a couple of endings which make sense or allow a grammatical sentence to be formed. Make sure that both grammar and meaning are respected in the answers you have formed! Once you have narrowed down the possible answers, make your final decision in conjunction with the text.

3/6 There is only one possible answer on offer (even ignoring the text).

Task	Answer	Mark

4 *laufen* is used here in the sense of *gehen*, **not** 'to run'.

8 This is not stated in the text but is deduced with common sense.

9/10 For good German, these sentences need a *dann* in the subordinate clause, so the endings must fit in here. Having worked that out, it should be obvious which of the two sentences requires which ending.

At the end you should check whether the unused ending C is not ratified by the text. You surely realised that *Schwester* here is a nursing sister, not a relative of the old people!

There is a composition linked to this Reading stimulus in the Mixed Skills unit.

F	**1**	vereinbaren		1
	2	dynamische		1
	3	Büro		1
	4	aufzieht		1
	5	Ausrüstung/Technologie		1
	6	Wohnzimmer		1
	7	vierjährigen		1
	8	Arbeit		1
	9	Vortrag		1
	10	langsamen		1
	11	selbständig		1
	12	denken		1
	13	etabliert		1
	14	erfahrenen		1
	15	besprechen		1

Examiner's tip **1** Take this verb meaning 'to combine' from the adjective *vereinbar* at the end of the second sentence.

2 Clearly only an adjective would fit in here, and only this one is used in the text to describe Frau Peltzer – at the start of the second paragraph. Other words which you can lift from the text are not explained in the rest of these tips.

4 You will find in the same sentence as for Question **2** *zieht ihre beiden ... Kinder auf*. You simply have to recognise the separable verb and remember to join it up to end the given sentence.

5 The past participle *ausgerüstet* (= equipped) in the middle of the second paragraph gives you the clue to this.

8 The given sentence is based upon the start of the third paragraph, but the word you need to insert is based upon an understanding of the previous paragraph. *Arbeit verrichten* = to carry out work.

10 This comes from *im kleinen Gang* – third paragraph.

13 Taken from *ein Standbein im Beruf zu schaffen* = to be on a firm footing in one's career.

Task		Answer	Mark

14 Derived from the noun *Erfahrungsaustausch* in the last paragraph: *erfahren* = experienced.

15 A tester: you must interpret the final sentence.

There is a composition linked to this Reading stimulus (and to Reading Task N and Listening Task R) in the Mixed Skills unit.

G(i)	**1**	das Gute zusammen mit dem Schlechten wegwerfen	**3**
	2	mit lauter Stimme	**2**
	3	sie haben es satt, Faxe zu schicken	**3**
	4	das Nützliche vom Unnützlichen unterscheiden/entscheiden, was nützlich und unnützlich ist	**2**

Examiner's tip

Vocabulary for the whole text:

in grauer Vorzeit	= in the dim and distant past
der Reißverschluß	= zip
die Bon-Rolle	= receipt roll
stöhnen	= to groan/moan
quellen	= to pour/stream
beträchtlich	= considerable
die Anschaffungskosten abarbeiten	= to redeem the cost of buying
der schlichte Unfug	= pure nonsense
aufgeblasen	= puffed-up (as in image of bullfrog, *der Ochsenfrosch*) or self-important
eine Bereicherung	= a boon/blessing
eine zeitliche Verknappung	= a shortening of time
die Blubberei	= gabbling
die Kennung	= fax signal
sich entlarven	= to be exposed/revealed
die Zärtlichkeit	= tender word

It helps to have a fair idea of what the proverbs in **1** and **4** mean before seeing how they fit into the context. Try to use as many of your own words as possible, but make sure your German is accurate and that your explanation is clear.

G(ii)	**1**	Elend	**1**
	2	widersprüchlich	**1**
	3	Volumen	**1**
	4	Porto	**1**
	5	brandeilig	**1**
	6	Exemplare	**1**

Examiner's tip

Although the rubric states 'words or phrases', you need only one word for each. Don't be tempted to lift other words which are next to the corresponding word in the text in the hope of making the meaning clearer. This will cause confusion and lose marks. Make sure you copy/spell properly!

There is a composition linked to this Reading stimulus in the Mixed Skills unit.

Reading answers

Task	Answer	Mark
H(i) 1	Her already limited personal freedom (1) would be further reduced (1) if the father had more rights (1).	3
2	He doesn't understand what right we have (1) to keep the father away from the child (1) unless it is necessary (1).	3
3	A man who is at all concerned (1) about his child's welfare (1) will make an effort to treat the mother decently (1).	3
4	Further progress in genetic engineering will have to be made (1) before the mother is eliminated from the process of childbirth (1). Until that happens, men will have to put up with the inconvenience of having a woman, if they want a child (1).	3

Examiner's tip There is no need to translate the sentences word for word, but you must convey the full meaning **in the context**. The line references are there to help you locate the sentences. It is advisable to check the sentence before, and if necessary the sentence after, in the passage to see if these shed any light on the one you are explaining.

1 A crucial word here is *dadurch*. To render its true sense here you must go back to the previous sentence in the passage.

2 Don't miss *ohne Not*.

3 The sentence which follows this one in the text will give you a clue about what *mit Anstand* might mean, if you are stuck.

4 Be careful not to get this one back to front: the plural sie in the final clause refers back to *Männer* (not to the singular *die Mutter!*). Cheryl is looking at it from the man's point of view, not the woman's. Note her sarcastic tone.

Task	Answer	Mark
H(ii) 1	Nachdem er sich von der Mutter getrennt hatte (1), hat der Vater ihr nicht geholfen (1), ihr Leben neu aufzubauen (1).	3
2	Beide Eltern sind für die Entwicklung eines Kindes lebenswichtig (1). Genau das ist aber dem Kind versagt (1), weil der Vater kein Recht hat, sein Kind zu sehen (1).	3
3	Sie bedauert sehr, daß sie mit ihrem siebten Lebensjahr von ihm getrennt wurde (1). Deshalb will sie die einflußreichen Erfahrungen, die sie mit ihm gemacht hat (1), wieder ins Bewußtsein bringen (1).	3
4	Sie möchte, daß Männer ihre Rolle als Vater anders verstehen (1) und sich bewußt werden, daß sie mit der Zeugung ihren Anteil an einem neuen Menschenleben noch nicht vollendet haben (1), sondern, daß sie weiterhin Verantwortung für das aufwachsende Kind übernehmen müssen (1).	3
5	Ein Vater, der nicht mit der Mutter und dem Kind zusammenlebt (1), würde der Erziehung des Kindes nur schaden (1), wenn er mehr Rechte hätte (1).	3

Examiner's tip It is important not to lift key words or whole phrases from the text. The instructions are to paraphrase in **your own words**.

1 Lines 1–5. Try turning the nouns *Trennung* and *Hilfe* into verbs.

2 Lines 21–27. You should convey the overall situation here rather than render each line.

Task	Answer	Mark

3 Lines 58–69, but remember you only need 3 points. Some key words to paraphrase are: *prägend* + *Erlebnisse*, *austauschbar* or *nicht wegzuschneiden*.

4 Lines 73–78. Replace *Zeuger* with *zeugen*. For the idea of *materielle Versorger* you could use *Geld ausgeben*.

5 Lines 86–91. Try to do this on your own now! If you feel really confident, in your paraphrase of *Er würde nur die Entwicklung des Kindes stören*, try to keep the conditional using *würde* but follow it up with a *wenn* clause including the imperfect subjunctive.

I(i)	**1**	Die Leute sollten daran denken, wie die Produkte verpackt sind.	**1**
	2	Der Müll wird zum größten Teil weggeworfen (1). Dann wird er zum Müllberg (1).	**2**
	3	In Österreich wirft der Durchschnittsbürger pro Jahr 300 Kilogramm Müll in den Mülleimer.	**1**
	4	Weil es die Luft verschmutzt.	**1**
	5	Altglas kann man völlig (1) wiederverwenden (1).	**2**
	6	Weil man nur die Hälfte zum Recycling bringt (1). Der Rest geht in den Mistkübel (1).	**2**
	7	Es gibt mehrere Kunststoffsorten, die nicht unterscheidbar sind (1). es gibt kein System für die Wiederverwendung bereits gebrauchter Kunststoffe (1).	**2**
	8	Man kauft um 30 Prozent weniger Flaschen, die wiederverwertbar sind (1). Stattdessen kauft man Plastikflaschen (1).	**2**
	9	Aludosen sind zweckmäßig und nicht schwer (1), aber man braucht viel Energie und Wasser, um sie herzustellen und zu verarbeiten (1), so daß sie die Umwelt mehr schädigen als Mehrweg-Glasflaschen (1).	**3**
	10	Sie können die Industrie nötigen, Produkte anzufertigen, die für die Umwelt freundlicher sind (1), damit man Müll vermeidet (1).	**2**
	11	Die Konsumenten haben die Erzeuger gezwungen, FCKWs als Treibgas in Sprühdosen zu ersetzen (1). Sie könnten denselben Zwang in anderen Sphären ausüben (1).	**2**

Examiner's tip Note the instruction to use your own words as far as possible.

1 (Refer to lines 1–2). The noun *Verpackung* can be changed into a verb.

2 (Refer to lines 2–5). Try to use as many words given to you in the text but not those found in the same sentence which you are manipulating for the answer. Exchange *Abfallberg* given to you here for *Müllberg* (line 28). An active construction *Die meisten von uns werfen unseren Müll ...* has been changed into a passive one: *Der Müll wird ... weggeworfen*.

3 (Refer to lines 6–7).

4 (Refer to lines 7–8). Use synonyms of *verpesten* – e.g. *verunreinigen/ verschmutzen*.

5 (Refer to line 9). *Wieder ... einsetzen* could be replaced by *wiederverwenden* or *wiederverwerten* (which you can steal from Question **6**). Alternatively, use

Task	Answer	Mark

wiederverwertbar sein (line 7). Here a passive construction *Altglas könnte wieder ... eingesetzt werden* has been turned into an active construction with *man*: *Altglas kann man ... wiederverwenden.*

6 (Refer to lines 11–12). *Mistkübel* is taken from line 3. The Germans have borrowed our word for recycling (line 13).

7 (Refer to lines 13–15). The verb *unterscheiden* can be turned into an adjective: *unterscheidbar.*

8 (Refer to lines 16–18).

9 (Refer to lines 23–27). The nouns *die Herstellung* and *die Verarbeitung* can become verbs. Other synonyms: *brauchen* for *benötigen*, *schädigen* for *belasten*, and *zweckmäßig* for *praktisch.*

10 (Refer to lines 30–31). Synonym: *nötigen* for *zwingen*. Break the adjective *umweltfreundlich* down into its constituent parts *Umwelt* and *freundlich* and put them in a relative clause describing *Produkte*: *Produkte, die ...*

11 (Refer to the last two sentences). Be careful to distinguish this question from Question **10**. You have already explained **how** consumers can change matters, now show why they can be successful. Synonyms: *Sprühdosen* (the original German word) for *Spraydosen* (taken from English); *Zwang* (*ausüben*) for *Druck*; *Sphäre* for *Bereich*. The passive *So wurde das Verbot ... durchgesetzt* has been changed into an active sentence with the subject *die Konsumenten*, in order to answer the question directly.

I(ii)	1	Flaschen, die man mehrmals verwenden kann	2
	2	ein Problem/Laster, das man erst später entdeckt	2
	3	unter dem Druck der Allgemeinheit/Gesellschaft	2

> **Examiner's tip**
>
> If you have coped with Part (i), this should not be too difficult. Clearly you need to find synonyms for the words in italics. For **2/3** this will mean using an additional phrase to explain their meaning, as there is no single word that could be a direct equivalent. For **3** there are a few individual words that fit. Avoid *das Publikum*: it means 'public' but in the sense of 'audience' – its German synonym would be *Zuhörer/Zuschauer.*
>
> There is a composition linked to this Reading stimulus (and that of Task J, and to Listening Task L and the oral examination on the CD/cassette Sections 3/4) in the Mixed Skills unit.

J(i)	1	Die Vorteile sind, daß der Verkehr sicherer wird (1) und besser fließt (1), und die Umwelt weniger belastet wird (1).	3
	2	Die CO_2-Emissionen (bis zum Jahr 2005 um 25 Prozent) zu reduzieren. (One mark only if bracketed material is omitted.)	2
	3	Man brauchte eine Liste von Maßnahmen, die man treffen/ergreifen könnte.	1
	4	Es ist nötig, die Energiepolitik zu ändern (1) und bessere Kraftanlagen zu bauen (1).	2
	5	Im Falle des Autoverkehrs, wo der Ausstoß des Kohlendioxids verringert (1) oder zumindest stabilisiert werden muß (1).	2

Task	Answer	Mark
6	Statt mit der Bahn zu fahren, (1) fährt man mit dem Auto (1).	2
7	Die Einwohner der Industrieländer (1) müssen ihr Benehmen verändern (1).	2

Examiner's tip Sections 3 and 4 of the oral examination on the CD/cassette deal with similar aspects of the topic and help with some vocabulary.

1 (Refer to line 3) Break up *Verkehrssicherheit* into *Verkehr + sicher*, *Verkehrsfluß* into *Verkehr + fließen*; change *Belastungen* into the verb *belasten* and introduce a passive instead of an active construction.

2 (Refer to lines 5–7) As for Task I, synonyms can be found in the text itself: for *der Ausstoß des … Kohlendioxids* use CO_2*-Emissionen* (line 10). You should know *reduzieren* to replace *verringern*. As an alternative you could lift from the text *eine* CO_2*-Minderung* (line 14), adding *erreiche*n. Dates and statistics have really to be left as they are, although *ein Viertel* has been converted to a percentage in the answer.

3 (Refer to lines 8–9) Use *Maßnahmen treffen*.

4 (Refer to lines 9–11) *Umbau* could be turned into a verb; synonym: *Kraftanlagen* for *Kernkraftwerke*.

5 (Refer to lines 13–15). Use *der Austoß des Kohlendioxids* and *verringern* not used in **2**. See how you can switch material from the text around!

6 This refers back to the sentence preceding it in the text.

7 (Refer to the final sentence) Synonyms: *Länder* for *Staaten*; *Benehmen* for *Verhalten*. Turn *Veränderung* into a verb.

Task		Answer	Mark
J(ii)	1	eine Höchstgeschwindigkeit [auf Autobahnen einführen]	1
	2	Hier handelt es sich darum	1
	3	[Wenn das nicht] geht	1
	4	auf die Bahn (1) anlocken (1)	2

Examiner's tip Proceed as for Task I Part (ii). In **1–3** you need to replace only one word – *darum* can be left in your answer to **2**. However, in **4** you need to find an equivalent of *Schiene* and of *locken*.

There is a composition linked to this Reading stimulus (and to Listening Task S) in the Mixed Skills unit.

There is also a composition linked to this Reading stimulus and that of the previous Task (I) in the Mixed Skills unit.

K (*Töpfer*) In the old German states/ two people share a car,/ in the new states four did so./ A catching up process/ is taking place over there,/ which does not represent/ any long-term outlook/ – that can only occur if we alter our pattern of behaviour./

I can perfectly well imagine,/ that we will no longer fly/ to the next summit meeting/ but will be brought together/ via a screen./ Unfortunately the American President did not talk in Rio, for example,/ about such changes to our everyday life.

for whole task = **15**

Reading answers

Task	Answer	Mark

der Aufholprozeß = catching up process
langfristig = long-term
per Bildschirm = via a screen
der Alltag = everyday life

Remember what was said in the introductory advice at the beginning of this unit about translation technique. If you need to write each bit of the sentence down in English as you read through it, you must then make sense of this rough version.

For example, if you translate the first sentence of the second paragraph word for word you get: I can perfectly well imagine/that we/to the next summit meeting/no longer/with the plane travel. Similarly, literally translated the last sentence comes out: about such changes to our everyday life/for example/the American President/in Rio/unfortunately/did not talk. Try putting these jigsaw pieces into a normal English sentence. When you have finished, give yourself one mark for each section shown above which is perfectly correct. As with Tasks L, M and N, there are sometimes different ways of expressing the text in English, so allow yourself credit, if you have found a valid synonym, provided your answer reads like good English.

L If sister Marlis is there,/ she (the old lady) has somebody to talk to for half an hour./ She speaks of her life,/ of the time when there were cows and pigs on the farm,/ when the land had to be worked/ and the vineyard tended./ She loves to talk about her children,/ about the only daughter who has emigrated,/ about the married son who lives in Bavaria,/ and of course the two sons living at home./ A close relationship exists/ between the married couple and the nursing sister,/ 'who somehow is almost one of the family'./

In the meantime she (sister Marlis) has sat the old man down to breakfast at the kitchen table./ Time is pressing./ At any rate 15 to 20 old people want/ to be looked after between 7 am and 1 pm./ For some the qualified nurse must take out catheters (tubes)/ and administer injections,/ others have to be washed and put into clean beds.

for whole task = **20**

Refer to the vocabulary given for Task E. Having completed that task and having worked through Task K, you should be able to cope without further help here. When you have completed the work, mark as for Task K.

M So really important,/ extremely urgent communications,/ that come like lightning,/ invitations or manuscripts/ are merrily mixed up with mere nonsense,/ with expressions of opinion/ and idealistic suggestions to make the world a better place/ that are puffed up like bull frogs with their self-importance,/ and with other smart faxes/ to go straight into the wastepaper bin./ Do fax operators really not have any voluntary self-control?/ I mean something like this:/ the quick fax is like so many other things in our time a blessing/ which also brought with it a shortening of time/ (– in that respect not unlike the computer, our slave and boss).

Task	Answer	Mark

Faxing is unsuited to/ only two types of communication previously carried out by letter./ These are love letters and anonymous pieces of writing./ The most terrible, shameful specimens/ of cowardly opinion babbling/ would be given away at any time/ by the sender's fax signal./ That's a good thing./ The exchange of tender words by fax/ is also ruled out for various reasons.

for whole task = **25**

Examiner's tip

Refer back to the vocabulary for Task G.

Taken word by word the first sentence reads:

So/are mixed up/merrily/really important, extremely urgent/lightning-like communications, invitations or manuscripts/with mere nonsense/, with bullfrog-like/puffed up expressions of opinion and world improving (idealistic) suggestions/straight for the wastepaper bin.

Now polish this up to convey the meaning behind the image of the bloated bullfrog and to render it in better style: you will have to put some adjectives (e.g. lightning-like/bullfrog-like/world improving) into clauses beginning with 'which/that' (e.g. 'that come like lightning') or an infinitive (e.g. 'to improve the world'). Apply the same principles – of bringing out the full sense of the passage with good English turns of phrase – to the rest of the task. When finished, mark as for Tasks K and L.

N

In families with children and gainfully employed mothers/ the housework is to a large extent left to women./ In households with two wage earners and children/ an equal sharing of work as in a partnership/ apparently founders through men's lack of willingness/ to take an appreciable share of the work off women.

Fathers of families are occupied/ for roughly 2 hours a day with domestic chores,/ such as repairs, gardening and vehicle maintenance./ In the traditionally feminine area of work they take part only/ in shopping and looking after the children.

The daily routine of housework – cooking, washing up, cleaning and doing the washing/ – is left, however, to a large extent, to the mothers and women./ Statisticians calculate the time that gainfully employed mothers spend/ on housework to be on average five to six hours a day.

for whole task = **15**

Examiner's tip

erwerbstätig	= gainfully employed
weiterhin/weitgehend	= to a large extent
gleichmäßig	= equal
scheitern	= to founder/fall down/fail
fehlend	= lacking/missing
wesentlich	= substantial/considerable/appreciable
lediglich	= simply/merely

A poor translation of the first sentence – based on taking each word at its individual meaning – would run:

Activities in the household remain in families with children and gainfully employed mothers to a great extent to women left up to.

Task	Answer	Mark

You should by now be able to spare the examiner this sort of nightmare. Having worked through the preceding translation tasks, you will have realised the importance – stressed in the introductory advice at the beginning of this unit – of re-reading your version in order to tidy it up and deal with any omissions. Mark it as for the previous translation tasks.

There is a composition linked to this Reading stimulus (and to Reading Task F and Listening Task R) in the Mixed Skills unit.

Task	Answer	Mark
O	(In Saxony) in 1980, 71,000 babies were born	1
	whereas in 1992 only 25,000 born.	1
	The Prime Minister called it a demographic revolution.	1
	The population was unaware of it.	1
	One can accept it.	1
	Let the situation drift;	1
	encourage immigration of young people	1
	or (encourage) pregnancy.	1
	Otherwise by 2030 those over 60/retired/pensioners	1
	will be one third of the population.	1
	Currently they are one fifth;	1
	Western birth rate is constant;	1
	Eastern birth rate is falling.	1
	In 1989 the West produced 11 births per 1000,	1
	the East (produced) 12 per 1000.	1
	Saxon Social Minister calls it 'worrying'.	1
	Reliable analysis about the causes is lacking.	1
	Regional differences are not recorded in any detail.	1
	Eastern midwives are less busy since 1989.	1
	There is little prospect of economic upturn	1
	but high prospects of unemployment and emigration.	1
	SED family policy is now having an effect.	1
	In the 1970s they allowed abortion and introduced new contraception.	1
	The pill caused birthrate to fall	1
	five years after the West's	1
	partly caused by a lack of young mothers	1
	and emigration	1
	but there are subjective causes.	1
	Because of the economic crisis people are not having children	1
	or are delaying having them.	1
	Social Minister Geißler is not optimistic about financial inducements	1
	but (he) is arguing for tax inducements and payments for mothers to (return to) work.	1
	Pregnancy should be no barrier to women working.	1
	He also praises the sound of babies as a sign of life.	1
	He attacks/calls sterile an individualistic society where children are avoided.	1

Task	Answer	Mark

Examiner's tip

einer Sache bewußt sein	= be aware of something
sich auf etwas einstellen	= to accept something
alles treiben lassen	= let things drift
einwandern	= to immigrate
der Anreiz (-e)	= incentive
der Säugling (-e)	= baby
beunruhigend	= worrying
verläßlich	= reliable
oberflächlich	= superficial
die Hebamme (-n)	= midwife
der Aufschwung	= economic upturn
die Abwanderung/der Wegzug	= emigration
die Abtreibung	= abortion
das Verhütungsmittel (-)	= contraceptive
der Pillenknick	= slump in birthrate caused by the pill
die Delle am Lebensbaum	= dent in the tree of life
verschieben	= put off/postpone
der Nachwuchs (no plural)	= offspring/children
die Schallgrenze	= sound barrier/limit to which one can go
die Steuerfreibetragsgrenze	= lower earnings limit (after which tax has to be paid)
der Lohnzuschuß (-üsse)	= pay subsidy
verbauen	= block/obstruct
prangern	= to pillory/offer to public ridicule
unfruchtbar	= sterile

There are 35 scoring points from which you need 30. Take great care over figures, as it is easy to make a little slip and lose a whole mark. By all means start – as suggested in the introductory advice to this unit – by jotting down in note-form each important point as it occurs to you on reading through the passage. You should then be able to write your notes out in continuous prose containing 30 points without exceeding the 210 word limit. Once you have finished your attempt, notice how the suggested answer, although broken down into individual points for you to mark your work, keeps to these set rules. It can be read continuously and would be slightly less wordy still if the points did not have to be given separately for your benefit. If you tried to translate the first paragraph and then compared the translation to the first eleven points given in the suggested answer, you would notice how much of the text is redundant. By translating you use almost twice as many words.

P	There will be no new Government programme for job training in the East.	1
	German industry and commerce (= 'it' in points below) has promised to increase the number of training vacancies	1
	with a proportionately greater increase in the new German states.	1
	So far it has increased the apprenticeships by 2%.	1
	The Education Minister (Jürgen Rüttger) has reminded it that 8% are outstanding.	1
	He thinks that 140,000 vacancies are needed,	1
	12,000 more than last year.	1
	65% of vacancies are subsidised by the Federal Government (including Employment Ministry) and the States.	1

Task	Answer	Mark
	Last year 14,500 additional private apprenticeships were financed by this common initiative.	1
	According to the Minister 1700 of these have not yet been taken up.	1
	This initiative costs 860 million Marks of which the Federal Government pays half.	1
	The Government calculates that 480,000 vacancies will be needed in the West in 1996	1
	and more than 490,000 in 1997.	1
	The Government will make its own contribution this year.	1
	At least 5% more apprenticeships will be offered in the Civil Service.	1
	The Minister now sees it as the responsibility of the States and the local Authorities to act.	1
	They have not given firm figures.	1
	They must do so if they are to show that they do not want to shirk their responsibility.	1
	Only a third of firms were training apprentices.	1
	The Government wants to put a package of measures together with employers and trades unions	1
	to make smaller firms more willing to offer training.	1
	States must organise more flexible teaching in vocational schools.	1
	A training 'year' at these schools before apprenticeship should include only 6 months' training.	1
	Anyone over 18 should go back to his work on a day set aside for training at vocational school.	1

Examiner's tip Vocabulary (meanings given in context)

die Wirtschaft	= industry and commerce
die Zusage	= commitment/promise (cf verb *zusagen*)
verabschieden	= to adopt/to pass
anheben	= to increase
ausstehen	= to be still to come
mahnen	= to remind
außerbetrieblich	= private
erforderlich	= required
die Bundesverwaltung	= Civil Service/Government Administration
die Kommune (-n)	= administrative district within a *Land*
in den Betrieb gehen	= go to work

There are 24 scoring points from which you need 20. This is a much denser text than Task O, so there is less redundant material. Some points are made more quickly in German with its compound nouns, so you have to prune back in other places.